The Fundamentals of Architecture
Lorraine Farrelly

ava
academia

An AVA Book

Published by AVA Publishing SA
Rue des Fontenailles 16
Case Postale
1000 Lausanne 6
Switzerland
Tel: +41 786 005 109
Email: enquiries@avabooks.com

Distributed by Thames & Hudson (ex-North America)
181a High Holborn
London WC1V 7QX
United Kingdom
Tel: +44 20 7845 5000
Fax: +44 20 7845 5055
Email: sales@thameshudson.co.uk
www.thamesandhudson.com

Distributed in the USA & Canada by:
Ingram Publisher Services Inc.
1 Ingram Blvd.
La Vergne TN 37086
USA
Tel: +1 866 400 5351
Fax: +1 800 838 1149
Email: customer.service@ingrampublisherservices.com

English Language Support Office
AVA Publishing (UK) Ltd.
Tel: +44 1903 204 455
Email: enquiries@avabooks.com

Second edition © AVA Publishing SA 2012
First published in 2007

ISBN 978-2-940411-75-7

Library of Congress Cataloging-in-Publication Data
Farrelly, Lorraine.
The Fundamentals of Architecture. / Lorraine Farrelly. p. cm.
Includes bibliographical references and index.
ISBN: 9782940411757 (pbk. : alk. paper)
eISBN: 9782940447350
1. Architecture. 2. Architecture -- Study and teaching.
3. Architectural design.
NA2500 .F37 2012

10 9 8 7 6 5 4 3 2 1

Design by Gavin Ambrose
Cover image: copyright of GuoZhongHua and courtesy of
Shutterstock.com.

Production by AVA Book Production Pte. Ltd., Singapore
Tel: +65 6334 8173
Fax: +65 6259 9830
Email: production@avabooks.com.sg

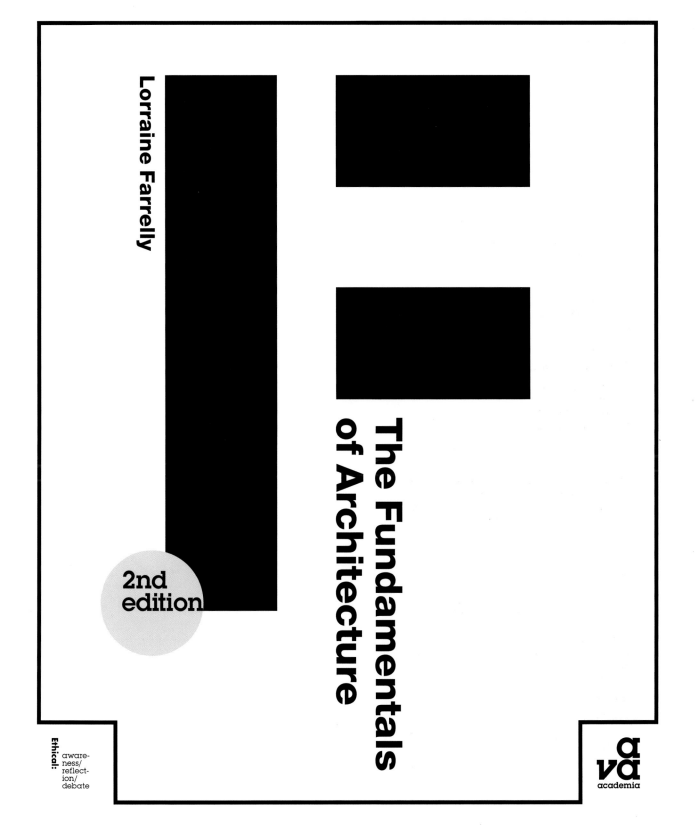

Lorraine Farrelly

The Fundamentals
of Architecture

2nd
edition

Ethical: aware-
ness/
reflect-
ion/
debate

ava
academia

Contents

4

CHAPTER 4

CHAPTER 5

CHAPTER 6

Introduction

Architecture
1. The art or practice of designing and constructing buildings.
2. The style in which a building is designed and constructed.

This second edition of *The Fundamentals of Architecture* introduces architecture to a wide audience. It will explore fundamental ideas that architects need to consider when designing buildings, places and spaces. The intention of this book is to introduce the fundamental principles of architecture. There are many visual references and illustrations that explain the thinking process required to develop an idea and, eventually, build a building.

Many architectural ideas are never realized; buildings require a vision and ideas can remain conceptual or stay on the drawing board. Architecture is a visual language and architects communicate through drawings, models and eventually through the spaces and places we construct.

This book has been divided into chapters that summarize various aspects of thinking during the process of designing buildings. This process starts with a concept or idea. This may be stimulated by an aspect of the brief – the intended function of the building. It may be an aspect of the material or construction of the building that inspires the concept, or some historical or contemporary precedent or existing building.

Architecture is a complex and compelling subject. Buildings surround us and make up our physical worlds. Making a building requires many layers of thinking and exploration.

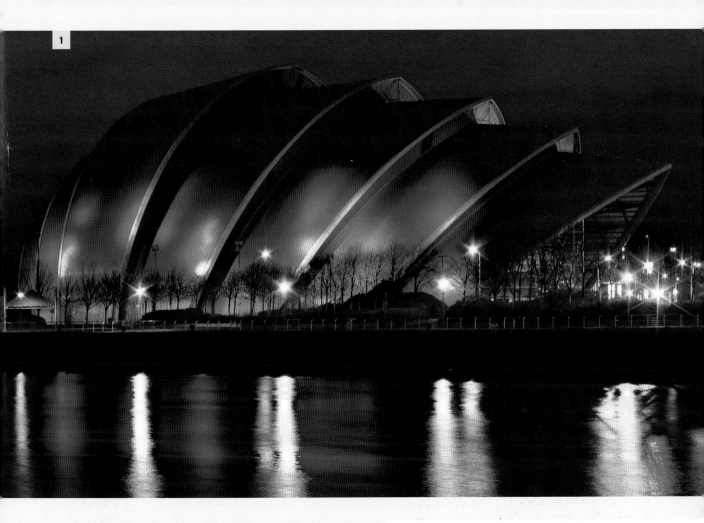

At its simplest, architecture is about defining the physical space around us, for example, a room and the objects within it. It can be a house, a skyscraper or a series of buildings, or part of a master plan of a city. Whatever the scale of the building, it evolves incrementally from concept sketch or drawing to inhabited space or building.

**1. SECC Conference Centre, Glasgow, Scotland
Foster + Partners, 1995–1997**
This building has a strong profile on its site along the River Clyde in Glasgow. The centre has a curved aluminium roof, which looks much like the hard shell of an armadillo, suggesting a strong, formal metaphor for the building's form and shape.

1. The Schröder House, Utrecht, The Netherlands
Gerrit Rietveld, 1924–1925
Artistic movements can also influence architectural form. The De Stijl (the style) movement in The Netherlands strongly influenced the development of Gerrit Rietveld's architecture, in particular his Schröder House in Utrecht.

2. Sketch of the Schröder House
This student drawing shows a geometric analysis of the Schröder House. When laid over an elevation drawing of the building, it shows how each element is proportionally connected. The red lines show the incorporation of the 'golden section' (see page 123), which is a geometric proportioning system.

CHAPTER BY CHAPTER

This book has been structured and divided into a series of subjects in order to cover the full design process.

The first chapter, Placing Architecture, refers to the site the building occupies and how that needs to be analysed and understood before starting the idea. The next chapter, History and Precedent, shows that all architecture is informed by ideas that have preceded it – this could be a reference to a plan, a use of material or a structural idea. No architecture is completely new; it connects to a vast knowledge of historical precedent, whether implicit or explicit, or informed by the recent and distant past.

The third chapter, Construction, introduces the basic aspects of building techniques. This chapter includes aspects of structure and material, and the making and substance of building.

The next chapter, Representation, refers to the communication of ideas, from freehand sketching, to computer drawing and modelling. The fifth chapter, Contemporary Ideas, explores the many ways in which architecture can be influenced by the prevalent 'zeitgeist', or spirit of the age.

The final chapter explores the realization of a building, from the first stages of conceptual thinking, through to the final stages of implementation of a building on site. This is where all the thinking, the consideration of the site, precedent, materials and structure come together. Making a successful building or structure requires the planning of information and organizing teams of professional people who do the facilitating and building contractors who do the making. The success of a building can be judged by the response of the client and how it fulfils its original brief.

3. Analysis of the Schröder House
This three-dimensional perspective drawing of the Schröder House suggests how the internal spaces of the building are defined by intersecting horizontal and vertical planes. The shadow projected at the bottom of the drawing directly connects to the building's plan.

Chapter 1
Placing Architecture

In architectural terms, 'context' generally refers to the place in which architecture or buildings are located. Context is specific and significantly affects how an architectural idea is generated. Many architects use context to provide a clear connection with their architectural concept, so the resultant building is integrated and almost becomes indistinguishable from the surrounding environment. Other responses may react against the environment, and the resultant buildings will be distinct and separate from their surroundings. Either way, the critical issue is that the context has been studied, analysed and responded to deliberately and clearly.

1. Townscape model
This model of a laser-cut map highlights aspects of a townscape: a project site is identified as a series of red blocks to distinguish it from the surrounding city site.

Site

Architecture belongs somewhere, it will rest on a particular place: a site. The site will have distinguishing characteristics in terms of topography, location and historical definitions.

An urban site will have a physical history that will inform the architectural concept. There will be memories and traces of other buildings on the site, and surrounding buildings that have their own important characteristics; from use of materials, or their form and height, to the type of details and physical characteristics that the user will engage with. A landscape site may have a less obvious history. However, its physical qualities, its topography, geology and plant life for example, will serve as indicators for architectural design.

There is a fundamental need for an architect to understand the site that a building sits on. The site will suggest a series of parameters that will affect the architectural design. For example, broad considerations might include orientation (how the sun moves around the site) and access (how do you arrive at the site? What is the journey from and to the building?).

The location of a building relates not only to its site, but also to the area around it. This presents a further range of issues to be considered, such as the scale of surrounding buildings and the materials of the area that have been previously used to construct buildings.

On site it is important to imagine ideas of form, mass, materials, entrance and view. The site is both a limitation to design and a provider of incredible opportunities. It is what makes the architecture specific and unique as no two sites are exactly the same. Every site has its own life cycle, which creates yet more variables in terms of its interpretation and understanding. Site analysis is critical for architecture, as it provides criteria for the architect to work with.

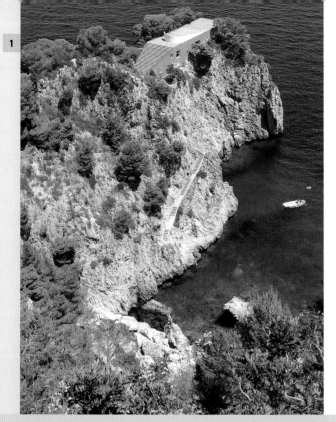

1. Casa Malaparte (Villa Malaparte), Capri, Italy
Adalberto Libera, 1937–1943
Adalberto Libera provides us with a clear example of a building responding to its landscape. The Casa Malaparte sits on top of a rocky outcrop on the eastern side of the Island of Capri in Italy. It is constructed from masonry, and is so intrinsically connected to its site that it actually appears to be part of the landscape.

2. A city skyline, London, UK
In an urban environment, a mixture of historical and contemporary buildings can work well together. The London skyline, viewed here from the South Bank, shows a city that has evolved over hundreds of years, each element connecting to the other in terms of material, form and scale.

1. Istanbul: Karaköy analysis
This is a map of an area of Istanbul, alongside the water edge, the study identifies the key centres of activity along the map and also describes the various intended 'character areas' through use of colour.

14 SITE ANALYSIS AND MAPPING

Techniques to record and understand a site are varied, from physical surveys (measuring quantitatively what is there) to qualitatively interpreting aspects of light, sound and experience. Most simply, just visiting a site to watch and record its life cycle can provide clues about how to produce a suitable design response.

Contextual site responses respect the known parameters of the site. Acontextual responses deliberately work against the same parameters to create contrast and reaction. For either approach it is necessary for the architect to have read the site, and properly understood it via various forms of site analysis.

To properly analyse a site it must be mapped, which means recording the many forms of information that exist on it. The mapping needs to include physical aspects of the site, but also more qualitative aspects of the experience and personal interpretations of the place.

There are a range of tools that can be used to map a site, investigate it and produce a design from its indicators. These are analytical tools that allow the site to be measured in a range of different ways.

Placing Architecture

2. Personal interpretations of a site
A collage image of London comprises a set of sketches of a journey, overlaid on a train map; a personal interpretation of a visit to London.

TOOL ONE: PERSONAL INTERPRETATION OF A SITE

The first impression we have of a place is critical. Our personal interpretations of the overall character of a site will inform subsequent design decisions, and it is important to record these honestly and immediately.

The idea of a personal journey around a site and the interpretation of it is something that Gordon Cullen focuses upon when he describes the concept of 'serial vision' in his book *The Concise Townscape* (1961). This concept suggests that the area under study is drawn as a map, and a series of points are then identified on it, each one indicating a different view of the site. These views are then sketched out as small thumbnails, which offer personal impressions of the site's space.

Serial vision is a useful technique to apply to any site (or building), in order to explain how it operates spatially and to identify its significance. The visuals can be created either as a series of sketches or as photographs of the journey, as long as they are assembled and read in sequence.

1., 2. & 3. Figure ground studies
1. Figure ground study of London with the River Thames clearly indicated as an open space.
2. A site in Old Portsmouth, UK; the blue areas indicate the water's edge, major roads are grey and the buildings are black.
3. This series of images illustrates the position of a site in relationship to its orientation.

TOOL TWO: FIGURE GROUND STUDY

A figure ground study is a type of drawing that maps buildings as solid blocks, clearly identifying the space around them. A figure ground study presents a city as areas of spaces and solids, producing an abstract site analysis. This method allows for a focus on the figure (building) and the ground (space around the building). Historically, figure ground studies have been used to identify the different types of space in cities.

Site analysis

Within the figure (handwritten annotations):
Possible extended site boundary
THE WOOLSTAPLERS
14.0m
Site Boundary
Ugly façade
County Library
Roman bath remains boundary
ars.
Division of site into the quadrants
Telephone Exchange
13.7m
Possible route through site
Roman access site
CHAPEL STREET
Barrier blocking/hiding buildings
TOWER STREET
El Sub Sta
CHAPEL ST
Main access route
1:500
Main access route

TOOL THREE: HISTORICAL TRACING OF THE SITE

Mapping a site over a series of significant stages in the course of its history provides a description of the life and memory of a place. Historical tracing can be achieved by overlaying a range of same-scale maps from the same site, each one depicting a different stage of the site's development. Doing so allows all the maps to be read concurrently and produces an image of the site that captures both its past and present.

Historical tracing can provide important triggers for a design idea. There may be a historic route, path, road or railway line that could suggest a significant axis, which could be acknowledged in a design idea. Similarly, remains of Roman walls or other important structures could also be recognized in a new building proposal. Historical site analysis can provide inspiration for a contemporary idea that connects directly with the past archaeology of a site.

4. Historical tracing of a site
Historical site mapping can bring together all the significant developments in a site's lifespan. This provides a 'complete' picture of the site, which can then be used as a source of inspiration for future concepts.

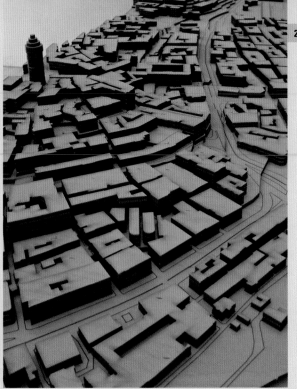

18   SITE SURVEYS

The condition of any site will need to be recorded in a survey. A survey can be described as a record of something already in existence, and can be produced either in the form of a physical map or model, or a measured drawing that explains where doors, windows or boundaries exist, as well as specific information such as relative heights of surrounding buildings, elevation details or heights of ground level across a site.

Detailed site analysis will measure physical aspects of the site. A site survey will provide dimensions of its width and depth and indicate any adjacent building at the levels of plan, elevation and section (see page 106) to create an accurate record of what currently exists. This is an essential part of the design process.

Site surveys can also record different 'levels'. A level site survey shows the variations of contours and inclines and these may also be used to suggest ways in which to develop the design concept.

1. Site surveys
A series of sketch urban studies of the town of Havant, UK, to illustrate the different types of spaces.

2. Massing model
A physical massing model of Istanbul indicating the density of the city.

3., 4. & 5. Combination images
These combination images use a digital aerial view and CAD model of a townscape.

3

4

5

Site > Place and space

Place and space

When does a space become a place? A space is physical, it has dimensions, it is located somewhere, it experiences change through time and it inhabits memory. A place is somewhere that activities, events and occasions happen. A building can be a place or a series of places. Equally, a city can be made up of many important spaces as well as being a place itself. A place has memory and some sense of identity.

THE MEMORY OF PLACE

The concept of memory of place is based on the premise that impressive places are strongly remembered; they have significant characteristics, sounds, textures, events that make them memorable. For architects, understanding the sense of place is particularly important when responding to, for example, a historic site or a building in a conservation area. There will be aspects of the history and the memory of the site that need to be reinforced.

Designing architecture and cities as places requires an understanding of the events that may take place, as well as the events that have already occurred. There is a need for imagined buildings or spaces that can be considered as arenas for these events to occur.

Carlo Scarpa 1906–1978
An Italian architect, Carlo Scarpa approached historic sites by placing his own contemporary architecture within an existing environment. He did this with great care and deliberation, using a range of forms and materials that are clearly identifiable from the existing building, yet still complementary. Scarpa carefully studied his site and respected important aspects of route, movement, view and reinforced these ideas with his own designs. In this way, he respected and explored aspects of the memory of the site.

1. Castelvecchio, Verona, Italy
Restoration by Carlo Scarpa 1954–1967
Castelvecchio (old castle) is a historic Italian castle and Scarpa's restoration transformed it into a relevant, contemporary piece of architecture. It can still be read as a castle, but also as a contemporary sculpture garden and museum.

2. La Villette Matrix from *Event-Cities* 2 (MIT Press, 2001)
Bernard Tschumi
In his book, *Event-Cities* 2, Bernard Tschumi explores the possibility of a city as a series of potential places for events (such as living, performing, buying or selling) to occur. These maps suggest the physical location of these events.

City context

The city is an environment in which much of our new architecture is placed. It is a context for living and working in contemporary society. The city provides precedent for architecture and an environment to interact with and enrich.

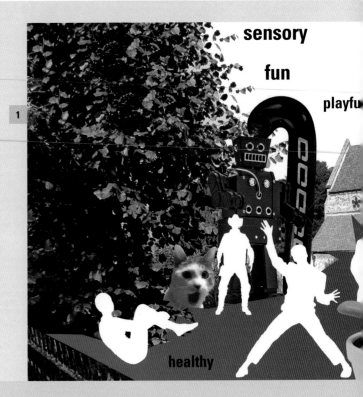

sensory

fun

playfu

healthy

A CREATION

Cities are places for events to occur and for life to unfold, they are constructs created by and engaged with thousands of people. Cities are imagined and depicted by many innovators, architects, politicians, artists, authors and designers.

There are many imagined views of the city. Many of these ideas represent a utopia of what a city could be and how we might live our lives. Realization of these ideals has been seen, to a certain degree, in Seaside in the US, Milton Keynes in the UK and Chandigarh in India. These new cities were first imagined and then created as new and complete concepts for living. Their design was not restricted by issues of historical infrastructure or a limited palette of available materials, instead there was an architectural opportunity to start afresh and build a new future.

energetic

engaging

inviting

community

activity

connecting

1. An interpretation of a church site
A collage image that uses a site photo as a basis for analysis with keywords and texts describing activity and potential for the site.

2. Parc de la Villette, Paris, France
Bernard Tschumi, 1982–1998
One of Parc de la Villette's 35 red follies (pavilions), which house cafés, information kiosks and other activity centres.

3. A student's impression of Istanbul
This series of sketches of Istanbul presents a personal view of the city, capturing people as well as places.

3

Landscape context

Within the context of landscape, buildings can either become part of the environment or distinct and separate from it. Many large buildings or structures can themselves be considered as types of landscape, such as airports, parks or mainline train stations. They are structures so large in scale that they contain buildings and other structures within them.

LANDSCAPE AND CONTEXT

A landscape, whatever its scale, creates new possibilities for dwelling, inhabiting and living. Whether a site is urban, open, closed or rural, in order for an architect to respond to it with a design proposal it needs to be understood, in both intuitive and personal ways, as well as through quantitative and measured assessment.

Together, these varying aspects of understanding provide important parameters to suggest an architectural solution, one that will be appropriate to the place and its meaning, and one that will contribute something to its context.

1. Madrid Barajas Airport, Madrid, Spain
Rogers Stirk Harbour + Partners, 1997–2005
Contemporary buildings, such as airports, exist at such a vast scale that they become in themselves a landscape. This airport shows the organic form that has been created within a landscape. The building's legible, modular design creates a repeating sequence of waves formed by vast wings of prefabricated steel. Supported on central 'trees', the roof is punctuated by roof lights providing carefully controlled natural light throughout the upper level of the terminal.

Redesigning a university campus

Project: Headington Campus, Oxford Brookes University

Architect: Design Engine Architects Ltd.

Client: Oxford Brookes University

Location/date: Oxford, UK/ 2009–ongoing

This chapter has considered the context of building, which requires a broad consideration of the site on which the building sits, as well as aspects of orientation, view, scale, massing and form, which are relative to the buildings and spaces around them.

When Oxford Brookes University decided to redevelop their main Headington campus, they commissioned British-based architects Design Engine to produce a new master plan for the 2,276 square meters (24,500 square feet) site. They were asked to design a series of interconnected buildings as part of a phased development for the university. Design Engine's plans were approved and work began on the £80 million (USD$123 million) scheme in 2011. The project encompasses a new library, student union and School of the Built Environment; all arranged around new internal courtyards, and commercial space leading off a new public piazza.

The challenge on this site was to work with a range of existing buildings and spaces on a scheme the scale of a village or small town. The brief for the project required an understanding of a range of buildings and spaces: some large, open spaces such as libraries; other smaller spaces, such as classrooms, seminars and complementary services spaces.

There will be a range of different scales and types of spaces for students to interact with each other, combining social space with group learning environments. These spaces will adapt to the students' changing needs and have the flexibility to enable both individual study and group learning.

In addition, there are open, external spaces as well as courtyards and internal squares. Finally, a range of spaces at the edge of the site are more public spaces; they form part of the streets and public space of the city and community around them. The spaces and buildings are part of a landscape, working together to create a new sense of place, a new campus environment and identity for the university. A set of streets and walkways are used to connect buildings, classrooms and other learning facilities for students.

1. Concept drawing
This three-dimensional concept drawing shows the relationship between the main elements of the project for the proposed campus and the route that connects the various different elements of the site.

The concept

The concept of the scheme is a linear connection through the site that links all the buildings and spaces. The main space or 'block' within the scheme is a library and student learning space, which will be clad with a specially treated glazing that will create a distinctive visual effect for the building. The idea of the building is that it forms a series of blocks and spaces. The wall of the buildings is analogous to a skin; a layer that brings together all elements of the site in a comprehensive visual way.

This 'skin' is comprised of cladding panels and a glazing system that has been purposely designed for the project. The building itself

will be a subject of aspects of research and investigation. The wall cladding and glazing system uses images of the cellular structure of trees to connect in a visual way to the university's environmental agenda, but also to bring nature into and onto the building.

This finish to the building will create a very distinctive effect; both internally, as it filters the light into the building and externally, as surface or façade.

1

1. Site diagram
This diagram indicates the existing building elements, the proposed elements and the new open spaces of the campus.

2. Master plan

An overall master plan view of the campus indicating
landscape, existing buildings and surrounding context.

Chapter 1

Exercise: Site analysis

Site analysis involves recording the aspects of a project site to inform the design as it develops. Each site is different and will have a different combination of considerations to record. It is important to take time to 'read' a site, to walk across and around it; to experience it and to try to record it in terms of physical information and data, such as size and orientation, but also more personal interpretation, such as interesting open spaces and important views. All this information can be referred to when designing to a project brief.

Site analysis should inform your site proposal. For this exercise:

1. Pick a chosen site and locate a site plan.

2. Tracing over the top of your site plan, indicate site issues that may influence your design.

3. Use diagrams to connect different issues across the site. Use different colours or shading to visually separate these ideas. There may be a series of diagrams that use the same base plan and concentrate on the key themes of the site.

Some issues that may affect your design:
Climate
Vistas
Existing axes
Transport
History
Scale
Existing structures
Material

1. Scale map
When analysing site context a scale map is important for understanding the location of a site and surrounding features. This base map can then be developed using colour and text to describe information about the site, such as wind direction, orientation and so on.

exercise

Key

	Site
	Sun path
	Wind
	Vistas
	Buildings
	Buildings of historical significance

Case study < **Exercise**

Chapter 2
History and Precedent

Design and innovation builds on precedent, on ideas and concepts that have evolved over time. Architecture uses precedents from social and cultural history and applies these influences to contemporary buildings, forms and structures. Having a historical understanding of buildings is an essential part of architectural design because it allows a relationship between the material, physical and formal developments that have been previously explored by other architects. Reacting against, or responding to, these ideas has been the basis of architectural evolution.

1. The Kolumba, Cologne, Germany
Peter Zumthor, 2003–2007
The Kolumba art museum, completed in 2007 by Peter Zumthor, responds and reacts to the existing historic context of a Gothic church. The new and old are physically connected.

3100 BC

Stonehenge in Wiltshire, England, is a monument made of a circle of stones. These sarsen stones weigh up to 50 tonnes each and originated over 50 km away. The structure is aligned with solstice and equinox points and is still used to celebrate these events today.

450 BC

The Acropolis in Athens, Greece, is a collection of buildings constructed on the Acropolis Hill. It consists of the Parthenon, Erechtheion and the Temple of Athena Nike. They represent the most enduring symbols of classical architecture and culture.

1194

Chartres Cathedral near Paris, France, represents a Gothic style of architecture and it achieves an impressive internal nave height of 37 metres (134 feet). Flying buttresses provide external support on the walls to help achieve this height.

1492

Leonardo da Vinci's Vitruvian Man represents the relationship between man and geometry. It was inspired by Da Vinci's studies of Vitruvius who described a set of measurements or modules based on man's proportions and dimensions.

1755

Laugier's hut (or the primitive hut) was described by Abbé Laugier in his seminal essay on architecture. It uses nature to create an analogy with architecture; the trunks of trees form columns, and branches and leaves form the roof. It represents the earliest and simplest form of shelter.

2600 BC

The pyramids at Giza in Egypt represent the most enduring of architectural symbols. Intended as tombs for the Pharaoh Cheops and his successors, they were built from stone and involved the organization of several thousand men to construct. The pyramids represent one of the most famous and wondrous monuments in the world.

AD 126

The Pantheon was built by the Roman emperor Hadrian and intended as a temple for all gods. He used concrete to create an impressive dome structure with an open oculus at the top that allows light to trace across the inner space.

1417

Filippo Brunelleschi was a Florentine architect who famously designed the Duomo in Florence, Italy. Brunelleschi developed a machine to allow perspective to be analysed and drawn. The machine was constructed from a series of mirrors that allowed him to analyse what he saw. Until this point, painting and images did not represent perspective accurately as there was no conceptual or mathematical understanding of it.

1779

Constructed from cast iron, the Iron Bridge in Shropshire, England, represents the industrial revolution and the new materials and technologies that were to revolutionize building form. Iron was to create the potential for lighter, more ambitious structures and buildings.

1919

The Bauhaus movement began its life as an art and architecture school in Weimar, Germany. It was directed by some of the most influential architects and designers of the twentieth century, including Walter Gropius, Hannes Meyer, Ludwig Mies van der Rohe and László Maholy-Nagy among others.

1924

Gerrit Rietveld designed the Schröder House in The Netherlands. It is the best-known example of De Stijl architecture and is a building that has no internal walls. The Schröder House was part of a philosophy that simplified visual composition to horizontal elements and the use of primary colours and black and white.

1947

Le Corbusier, who was interested in the idea of proportion, geometry and the human body, develops the modulor system. Le Modulor was published and used as a scale to design many buildings including the Ronchamp Chapel in France.

1851

Joseph Paxton built London's Crystal Palace for the Great Exhibition of 1851. Paxton introduced a new type of architecture, inspired by technology, engineering and innovation. Combining a lightweight iron frame with glass created a transparent piece of architecture.

2000

Marks Barfield Architects built the London Eye originally as a temporary structure to celebrate the millennium, but it has since become as celebrated a piece of architecture as the Eiffel Tower in Paris. It is a work of engineering and a dynamic piece of urban architecture at the same time, challenging our view of London.

1929

The Barcelona Pavilion was designed in 1929 by German architect Ludwig Mies van der Rohe. It represented a new type of modern architecture that questioned the position of walls, floors and roofs, and introduced a new vocabulary of planes and surfaces.

1931

Shreve, Lamb and Harmon designed the Empire State Building in New York. It was the highest frame structure of its time at 102 storeys.

1972

The Pompidou Centre in Paris, designed by Renzo Piano and Richard Rogers, reinvented the idea of the building as a machine. All the services, lifts, pipework and ventilation ducts were placed on the outside of the building for dramatic effect.

1889

The Eiffel Tower in Paris was built for the Exposition Universelle. Designed by engineer Gustave Eiffel, it was the tallest cast iron frame structure of its time. The tower was originally intended as a temporary structure, but now forms an important part of the city's identity.

1. The Pyramids at Giza, Egypt
c. 2600 BC
Pharaohs saw the building of these tombs as an expression of their reign, much as international corporations and governments of today build ever taller and more expensive buildings as symbols of their power and importance.

The ancient world
The history of architecture is intrinsically aligned with the history of civilization. While our nomadic ancestors had developed sophisticated forms of temporary shelter – some of which are still used today, such as the yurt tents of the peoples of the Mongolian plain – the change to a more sedentary form of existence fuelled the need for permanent shelter.

ANCIENT EGYPT

In contrast to the city states of Mesopotamia, which were often warring with each other, the Nile (in its final 1100 kilometres journey to the Mediterranean) was surrounded on either side by desert, and this made assault from the outside more difficult and resulted in a society that remained untainted by external influences for more than 3000 years. During this period the Egyptians developed architecture that was characterized in the early dynastic periods by pyramidal burial tombs formed above ground and, later, by the richly decorated tombs in the Valley of the Kings.

In both instances the buildings reflected the strongly held Egyptian belief in life after death. This belief was mirrored in everyday life too, and experienced as a series of dualities: night and day, flood and drought, water and desert. This belief and such dualities explain why the Valley of the Kings is located on the western side of the Nile, the horizon on which the sun sets, while the temples and settlements of Luxor are on the eastern side, the horizon of the rising sun.

This symbolic positioning of ancient Egyptian buildings was further enhanced by the precision with which they were constructed. The pyramids of Giza were built around 2600 BC, and are accurate to 100 millimetres (four inches) over their 150 metres (492 feet) perfectly square base, and the apex of the pyramid creates a precise geometric form derived from the golden section (see page 123). Within each pyramid, small passages running from the burial chambers are precisely aligned with celestial constellations, as these were seen as the resting place to which the soul of the pharaohs would travel in the afterlife.

The scale and exactness of these structures is breathtaking, and required, even by today's standards, an enormous feat of engineering, not least in sourcing the several million stone blocks used in their construction. These stones were quarried in Upper Egypt, some 640 kilometres (400 miles) from the site, and were transported by water before being raised into position.

NEOLITHIC STRUCTURES

The Stone Age is comprised of three periods, Palaeolithic, Mesolithic and Neolithic. Neolithic cultures created great stone structures in the landscape of the British Isles. Often forming large stone circles, these structures are impressive due to their scale, method of construction and the connections that they appear to have with the tracks in the sky of the sun and moon.

Stonehenge is probably the most well-known Neolithic structure. The stone circle formation on this site dates from around 3100 BC. Initially Stonehenge was a series of holes, commonly described as an 'earthwork'. This was superseded a thousand years later by the next stage of construction, which involved transporting the stones from the south-west coast of Wales. Stonehenge was not built out of necessity. It is not a construction concerned with shelter, but instead represents a spiritual connection with the natural and celestial worlds.

2. Newgrange megalithic tomb, Knowth, Ireland c. 3200 BC
This is the oldest solar conservatory in the world. A vast mound of rocks, stones and earth, Newgrange was built to celebrate the winter solstice sunrise, during which a shaft of light enters the heart of the tomb and illuminates its inner chamber.

3. Stonehenge, Wiltshire, UK c. 3100–2000 BC
Stonehenge is a Neolithic and Bronze Age megalithic monument. It is composed of earthworks surrounding a circular setting of large standing stones. Archaeologists think that the standing stones were erected between 2500 BC and 2000 BC although the surrounding circular earth bank and ditch have been dated to about 3100 BC.

3

The classical world

In architecture, the influence of Roman and Greek civilizations is found in the concepts, forms, ideas, decorations and proportions that have been reinterpreted as Renaissance (in fifteenth-century Italy), Georgian (in nineteenth-century London) and American colonial styles. There is an enduring sense of elegance and balance to classical architecture and ideas.

ANCIENT GREECE

While the civilizations of Mesopotamia and Egypt formed the foundations of architecture, it was in the societies of ancient Greece that the language of the discipline was first formalized.

Much of our modern culture finds its origins in the civilization of classical Greece. Political democracy, theatre and philosophy derive from a society that, having mastered the supply of food, found they had spare time to think, reflect and better understand the rules of the world around them. Some of the greatest minds in history, Plato, Aristotle and Pythagoras, laid down the patterns of thinking that would dominate Western culture for the next 2000 years.

The Hellenistic architecture of ancient Greece (produced during what is described as the 'golden period'), reached such refinement and quality that it subsequently earned its definition of 'classical'.

Today, reference to the classical language of architecture alludes not only to the form, but also to the way in which the architects of ancient Greece developed an architectural methodology that could be applied to all building types.

The literal building blocks of this methodology are the columns used to support the construction. These columns are in one of five forms, according to the slenderness and embellishment of their design. These forms are: Tuscan, Doric, Ionic, Corinthian and Composite, and rank in order from short and squat to slender and elegant. Collectively they are known as the five orders.

The diameter of each column not only determined its height, but also the space allowed between columns and therefore the overall ratio and proportions of the building it was supporting. Each individual element of Greek architecture had a mathematical relationship to every other element, making the building an integrated totality.

1. The five orders of classical architecture

The public buildings of the ancient Greeks and Romans were almost all designed using the five 'orders' of architecture. The orders are expressed according to the design of the column and the details of the upper parts of the façades carried by each. The five orders are shown here (from left to right): Tuscan, Doric, Ionic, Corinthian and Composite, and their designs range from simple and unadorned to highly decorative. The numbers in this diagram refer to the column's height/diameter ratio. For example, the Tuscan column's height is seven times its diameter.

THE FIVE ORDERS

TUSCAN   DORIC   IONIC   CORINTHIAN   COMPOSITE

This modular system, where the width of the column determined the proportions of the building, created a formula for design. This blueprint could be equally applied to a small house or a whole city and in so doing a connected and harmonious architecture could be created.

Many examples of ancient Greek classical architecture remain, and perhaps the best known is the Acropolis in Athens; the symbolic centre of the classical world. The Acropolis is effectively a fortified collection of individual buildings centred on the great temple of the Parthenon. This architectural icon was a place of worship housing a giant ivory and gold covered statue of the goddess Athene, patron of the city. Although few had the privilege to view the statue, the building's exterior was an expression of civic and national pride.

Its frieze, the band of sculpted panels that surrounded the building above the column line, is considered by many to contain some of the finest works of art ever made. The subject of much controversy, they are now housed in the British Museum and depict the Great Panathenaia, the four-yearly ritual robing of Athena, with such lifelike execution that solid marble seems to flow in the folds of material in the gods' gowns. This highlights the value that the Greeks placed in observation and understanding of the human form.

The classical world also devised urban planning. In cities such as Miletus and Priene, the social order was reflected in their houses and focal public buildings, assembly halls and gymnasia, which were all carefully laid out on a grid plan. Above all, their urban planning focused on the interchange of goods and ideas, and the 'agora' or marketplace might be considered the public heart of the Greek city.

In addition, the architects of ancient Greece produced great amphitheatres, able to accommodate an audience of 5000 with ease, providing perfect sight lines and acoustics, qualities that many architects find hard to emulate today.

The medieval world

The fall of Rome and the descent of western civilization into the cultural chaos that characterized the Dark Ages prompted a very different view of architecture from that which had existed in the classical world. In times of uncertainty, unsure as to his own abilities to understand the world around him, man often turns to external sources to govern the future. For this reason the medieval period saw a turn away from the secular towards the divine as a source of certainty.

GOTHIC ARCHITECTURE

The primary purpose of much medieval architecture was to communicate the biblical narratives to the largely illiterate masses. To serve this purpose, medieval cathedrals developed a unique form that reduced structural mass and allowed stained glass to illuminate the interior with the divine light and message of a Christian God.

In addition to this, the desire to escape the torments of earthly existence and seek solace in a heavenly realm brought about an emphasis on the vertical, resulting in an architectural style of ascension. Directing the eye heavenward, the Gothic style characteristically employed pointed arches and placed structure outside of the building. A great example of this is to be found in St Chappelle, close to the other great Gothic cathedral of Notre Dame, on the Isle de la Cité in Paris, France. A vertical architectural emphasis is seen on its exterior, with towering spires that once served as pilgrimage beacons (reflecting the belief that the taller the spire the greater the city's piety).

Gothic architecture also adopted a very precise and often complex geometric organization where sacred ratios (see page 123), echoed in the natural world, were employed as a celebration of the divine mind.

In domestic structures, the heights of the classical world were lost and Gothic architecture regressed to a largely vernacular type, using local ideas and materials and often based on timber-frame construction. While primitive in many respects, the overall results of the construction methods employed by medieval carpenters were of considerable technological ingenuity. The use of local materials in much of their natural form gave the buildings an intimate connection with their regional landscape and location. This is a characteristic that has recently been reinterpreted by the 'green' architecture movement.

In addition to this, the piecemeal development of towns and cities through the period produced irregular urban planning, which gave many towns a certain charm and sense of character. Towards the end of the medieval period, the re-emergence of secular concerns gave rise to more substantial structures based around trading activities. At the smallest scale, this was evident in the many market crosses erected in provincial towns, and at the other end of the spectrum, saw the construction of some of the finest medieval structures, including the Doge's Palace in Venice, Italy, which was one of the few secular constructions crafted to the level of a medieval cathedral.

1. Chartres Cathedral historical development
Emma Liddell, 2007
This diagram demonstrates how Chartres Cathedral has evolved from the construction of its early Gallo-Roman inner chapel (dated AD c.500), to the Gothic cathedral (dated AD c.1260) that we are all familiar with. Each new phase of building wraps around the previous one.

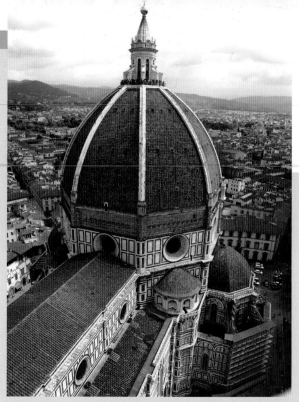

The Renaissance
Few times in the history of architecture show the sort of rapid and fundamental changes in attitude as was witnessed in Italy at the beginning of the fourteenth century.

HUMANISM

This period saw a rejection of medieval scholasticism and a revived interest in classical architecture. Those architects who had known Gothic building in Europe, but vividly remembered the great architecture of the Roman Empire, began to reconsider the classical language of architecture. This line of inquiry gathered pace in Florence, where wealthy, self-confident merchants and new banking families such as the Medici became patrons to a small group of architects who had started to revalue and tentatively experiment with the classical language of architecture.

To a previous generation, the works of the ancient classical world had seemed a form and complexity beyond experience. The new sensibility sought to understand classical architecture based on the validity of man's reasoning power and his ability to understand the world through observations and intellect.

Filippo Brunelleschi 1377–1446
Brunelleschi was born in Florence, Italy. He initially trained as a sculptor, before studying sculpture and architecture in Rome with Donatello. In 1418 Brunelleschi won a competition to design the Duomo of the Santa Maria del Fiore in Florence. His design was the largest dome over the greatest span of its time. Brunelleschi's Duomo is made up of a series of layered domes and the space between each is large enough to walk through. He was also responsible for inventing machines to assist with various aspects of architecture, from raising large weights to a better understanding of perspective.

Leon Battista Alberti championed this intellectual approach and set out the new discoveries of the classical world in his 1452 treatise *De Re Aedificatoria (On the Art of Building in ten books)*. In this he promoted the mathematical perfection of platonic forms as a mirror of God's divine perfection, and proposed that a centrally and symmetrically planned church would be more ideal than the familiar form of the Latin cross adopted in Gothic architecture. This ideal was only to take form some years later with Michelangelo's plans for St Peter's Basilica in Rome, which was testament to the power of Alberti's theoretical writing in architecture.

Perhaps one of the most potent symbols of the Italian Renaissance was **Filippo Brunelleschi's** dome of the Santa Maria del Fiore in Florence; the *Duomo*. Here the problem of spanning a 42 metre (138 feet) wide crossing required a solution for which history offered no precedents and Brunelleschi devised an ingenious method of banding the base of the dome with a giant iron chain in order to resist huge outward forces. Brunelleschi adapted the language of the Gothic church plan to produce a semi-circular arcade that was supported on classical columns at Santo Spirito, and used a similar form for the extraordinarily delicate arcade fronting the Foundlings Hospital in London. In this way he reinterpreted the classical language ingeniously, and adapted and modified the precedents he found in classical architecture to contemporary building typologies.

1. Santa Maria del Fiore (the Duomo), Florence, Italy
Filippo Brunelleschi, 1417–1434
This octagonal dome dominates the Santa Maria del Fiore. Brunelleschi drew his inspiration from the double-walled cupola of the Pantheon in Rome. The distinctive octagonal design of the double-walled dome, resting on a drum and not on the roof itself, allowed for the entire dome to be built without the need for scaffolding from the ground. This enormous construction weighs 37,000 tonnes and contains over four million bricks.

2. Façade of the Basilica di Santa Maria Novella, Florence, Italy
Completed by Leon Battista Alberti, 1456–1470
This building is unique because all its dimensions are bound to each other by the ratio of 1:2.

1

1. Piazza del Campidoglio, Rome, Italy
Michelangelo Buonarroti, 1538–1650
This space is designed as an elliptical courtyard. Michelangelo also designed the two buildings flanking the piazza to create a sense of increased perspective, exaggerating views across the city. The Piazza del Campidoglio has a centrepiece statue of the Roman emperor Marcus Aurelius. Michelangelo's piazza brings together geometry, route and monument in a coherent piece of urban design.

2. Sketches of Rome
Sketching the striking or intriguing buildings discovered when visiting a new city can be helpful in taking the time to study and understand their details and construction.

MICHELANGELO

As the Italian Renaissance developed, so the confidence of architects in their own creative powers grew. The late or High Renaissance saw Giorgio Vasari's *Le Vite de' più eccellenti pittori, scultori, ed architettori (Lives of the Most Eminent Painters, Sculptors, and Architects)* published in 1550. This book promoted the idea of the architect as a creative genius, an individual singled out for special powers beyond and above others.

Michelangelo felt that he had such creative powers and looked into his own imagination rather than drawing on outside precedents for inspiration. In so doing he was able to understand the classical language with a unique insight, which enabled him to both master and break its given rules. This is nowhere more evident than in his great entrance vestibule and staircase to the Laurentian Library in Florence.

Here Michelangelo questioned ideas that had previously been used in a very specific way in architecture. Not only did he split the pedimented entrance portal, thus questioning its historic structural role, but he also inverted the columns and cut them out of the wall.

Michelangelo moved architecture more towards the ornamental or illusory; his work was designed to evoke emotions and a feeling of theatricality. During this period the rebirth of classical architecture adopted mannerism (a style that was characterized by distortions in scale and perspective as well as a use of bright colour), and ultimately moved towards the opulence and decadence of the rococo, with buildings and civic spaces described as theatrical backdrops to the events of the city. This shift is no more evident than in Michelangelo's remodelling of the Capitoline Hill in Rome, which challenged the accepted rules of perspective and introduced buildings with competing elements of various scales within the same composition.

Baroque

The beginning of the eighteenth century witnessed a new age of reasoning. Copernicus, Kepler and Galileo overturned the established geocentric Christian cosmology and asked, if the earth and man were no longer at the centre of the universe, then what other established beliefs could be brought into doubt? This notion was met with an enormous burst of intellectual inquiry, which sought to establish new rules that would govern what was increasingly considered to be a 'clockwork' universe.

Claude Nicolas Ledoux 1736–1806
Ledoux was a French neoclassical (employing the original classical style from Greece and Rome) architect. He was involved in many monumental and visionary projects, such as the Royal Saltworks at Arc-et-Senans in France and the theatre of Besançon in France. Influenced by Greek classical architecture, Ledoux had ideas for a utopian city for a new society.

Étienne-Louis Boullée 1728–1799
Born in Paris, Boullée was involved in many of the city's large-scale symbolic buildings, including the national library. He also designed visionary structures that were never realized including the Cenotaph dedicated to Newton, which was a complete spherical structure. Boullée also wrote the influential essai sur l'art (essay on the art of architecture) (1794), which promoted neoclassical architecture.

1

RATIONAL BUILDING

Architecture too followed this pattern of inquiry with theorists such as Abbé Laugier seeking to establish the fundamental principles of the discipline by reducing the essence of building down to a primitive aedicule structure that, by extension, could be universally applied.

In practice, architects such as **Ledoux** and **Boullée** devised an architecture of purity that strived for the external truth of form. So-called rational building, derived from the rational philosophy of René Descartes, sought to build on the foundations of logical and deductive reason to produce an architecture based on indubitable premise. Boullée's proposals were of a giant scale and he built very little, but of those he did realize, his monuments to Sir Isaac Newton stand as a symbol of the age. Similarly, Ledoux's barrier gates for the city of Paris and his design for a radial city at Arc-et-Senans pre-empted much of the rational urban planning that would determine the future design of cities.

1. Symmetrical and rational plan of the Château de Versailles
This diagram shows the connection, along a central axis, between the gardens and the building of the Château de Versailles. Both plans are symmetrical along the axis. The château was designed by the architect Louis Le Vau and the gardens by landscape architect André Le Notre in 1661.

2. The Château de Versailles, Paris, France
Louis Le Vau, 1661–1774
Initially a small hunting lodge, The Palace of Versailles was extended by successive kings of France and designed to resemble its current form by Le Vau in 1661. It has been designed by architects and landscape architects and is an impressive connection of building and landscape, interior and exterior, by carefully considered views and axis.

The Renaissance < **Baroque** > Modernism

Inigo Jones 1573–1652
Born in England, Jones first studied classical architecture and then travelled to Italy. Heavily influenced by Andrea Palladio, who in the sixteenth century had interpreted original classical architecture in *I Quattro Libri dell'Architettura (The Four Books of Architecture)* (1570), Jones developed a Palladian style, which was an interpretation of classical architecture. In England, his most influential buildings are the Queen's House at Greenwich, the Banqueting House at Whitehall and the design of Covent Garden in London.

Sir Christopher Wren 1632–1723
Wren studied both astronomy and architecture at Oxford University. The Great Fire of London in 1666 gave him the opportunity to be involved in the rebuilding of the city.

He designed St Paul's Cathedral in London, was involved in the rebuilding of 51 of the city's churches and also designed Hampton Court Palace and Greenwich Hospital in the UK.

Nicholas Hawksmoor 1661–1736
Hawksmoor worked alongside Wren on St Paul's Cathedral, Hampton Court and Greenwich Hospital. He also assisted Sir John Vanbrugh on Blenheim Palace and Castle Howard in the UK.

Hawksmoor adopted the classical style and interpreted it to produce his own approach.

Rational building as a classical form reached the United Kingdom through the work of **Inigo Jones**, and the political revolutions that followed this intellectual revolution were brought into sharp focus outside the doors of Inigo Jones' Banqueting House, with the decapitation of Charles I.

Sir Christopher Wren remodelled much of London following the Great Fire of 1666 in this new enlightened fashion. The dome of St Paul's Cathedral and the surrounding spires by **Nicholas Hawksmoor** stood like beacons of intellectual clarity against the ramshackle irrational collection of timber-frame buildings that had characterized medieval London. Rational architecture brought a new scale and elegance to the city.

1

1. St Paul's Cathedral, London, UK
Sir Christopher Wren, 1675–1710
This current cathedral was constructed after its predecessor was destroyed by the Great Fire of London. The dome of St Paul's has a great physical presence on the skyline of London, and is an important visual feature and reference for the city.

However, as the eighteenth century unfolded, the rise of empirical philosophy in the United Kingdom brought an architecture that was the opposite of rational. The notion that truth was to be found through the senses (rather than through intellect) led to the first true landscape design of environments that were devoted to sensory excitation. **Lancelot 'Capability' Brown** devised gardens based on intrigue, variety and contrast, and Henry Hoare's gardens at Stourhead most vividly capture this concept.

2. Stourhead Garden, Wiltshire, UK
Henry Hoare II, 1741–1765
The design of the gardens at Stourhead is in stark contrast to the French ordered style that favours an axis for views and paths. Hoare's approach was to celebrate nature, and the Stourhead gardens are a contrived artificial landscape, making use of meandering paths to provide glimpses of important features such as the grottoes and follies contained within it.

Lancelot 'Capability' Brown
1716–1783
Lancelot 'Capability' Brown was an influential British landscape architect who worked on many important eighteenth-century country houses, aiming to complement their architecture through his landscape proposals. Brown began his career at Stowe in Buckinghamshire, and his work includes the gardens and estates of Blenheim Palace in Oxfordshire. His approach was to create a complete classical environment comprising a new landscape, lawn, trees, lakes and temples. The result was an illusion of a natural landscape, yet it was totally contrived as each piece had been carefully considered and placed.

Modernism

The beginning of the Enlightenment (or Age of Reason) had been accompanied by political revolution, but the modern world was initiated by another kind of revolution; that of industry. The development of steam power at the end of the eighteenth century changed what had been a predominantly rural population to an urban one and the cities at the heart of industry grew rapidly.

IRON AND STEEL

The new materials of the Industrial Revolution, such as wrought iron and steel, were quickly transferred into construction applications. This development marked a paradigm shift from bespoke, heavy, load-bearing construction to lightweight factory-produced building elements. The world celebrated the new products of mass production through a series of trade exhibitions. Most architecturally notable were those in London in 1851 and Paris in 1855. In London, the exhibition was housed in the enormous custom-built structure of the Crystal Palace.

Designed by **Sir Joseph Paxton**, the Crystal Palace used standard components of prefabricated cast-iron lattice, infilled with glass panels, to form a greenhouse of enormous proportions. Paxton's Crystal Palace used these newly available materials to their limit, borrowing traditional forms and structurally reinterpreting them.

In Paris, the properties of cast iron showed how lightweight construction could be employed to achieve previously unseen heights. The Eiffel Tower soared some 312 metres (1,023 feet) in the Parisian skyline and its skeleton frame was to be the forerunner of the tall buildings and skyscrapers that followed.

But the opportunity to show what could really be achieved fell to the US. In 1871 a fire destroyed much of the city of Chicago. Faced with a blank sheet for the city, architects again used the framing principle as a basis for construction but this time with steel, far stronger and proportionately lighter than iron. It was used to construct the first high-rise building in the world.

Louis Sullivan, credited with the phrase 'form follows function', was perhaps the first great architect of the modern age. His Carson, Pirie, Scott and Company Building, in Chicago, was a simple frame structure that allowed clear expression without decoration. This was a radical break from the classical ornamentation that had previously characterized much civic building.

Sir Joseph Paxton 1803–1865

Paxton was an English architect and keen gardener. His work at Chatsworth House in Derbyshire saw him experiment with framed glass structures that would allow him to grow and protect sensitive and delicate plants. From these, Paxton developed designs to build the Crystal Palace for London's Great Exhibition in 1851.

The project was the most innovative use of glass and steel at the time and was of an unprecedented scale. The Crystal Palace was intended to be a temporary structure, but was moved to Sydenham in South London after the exhibition had finished.

1. The Iron Bridge at Coalbrookdale, UK
Abraham Darby III, 1777–1779
The world's first cast-iron bridge was built over the River Severn at Coalbrookdale, England, by Abraham Darby III, and is now recognized as one of the great symbols of the Industrial Revolution. The bridge had a far-reaching impact on local society and the economy, as well as on bridge design and on the use of cast iron in building. It represents the new technology and engineering potential of the eighteenth century. The bridge translates the previous idea of a heavy stone structure into a light, elegant, almost transparent frame.

1

1

2

GLASS AND CONCRETE

Along with iron and steel, two other materials also came to characterize the modern movement: sheet glass and reinforced concrete. Ludwig Mies van der Rohe had seen the possibilities of new float glass production methods, which could create a material that would enable transparency and structural honesty and, it was believed, would herald a spirit of openness that was to mark the new utopian age of the twentieth century. Mies van der Rohe's Barcelona Pavilion design, an exposition building constructed in Catalonia in 1929, reduced the structure to a series of columns that supported a flat roof, with non-load-bearing partition walls made of glass and thin veneers of fine marble to divide the spaces within.

In conceiving architecture as a spatial continuity from inside to outside, Mies van der Rohe also broke the historic paradigm of the interior being a series of spaces enclosed by solid load-bearing walls and punctured by windows and doors. Instead, he produced an open plan in which space flowed seamlessly through the building, unhindered by the mass and solidity of the structure. His was the 'new' architecture: open, light and elegant.

Ludwig Mies van der Rohe 1886–1969
Born in Germany, Mies van der Rohe was part of the group that established the Bauhaus school (see page 144). He was an architect, teacher, furniture designer and urban planner, who questioned all aspects of design. Mies van der Rohe also questioned the idea of walls, floors and ceilings, reinventing architectural language to become planes and points.

Mies van der Rohe's significant buildings include the Barcelona Pavilion and the Seagram Building in New York. These buildings are two of the most important pieces of twentieth-century architecture in terms of their use of material and subsequent form.

1. Hedmark Museum, Hamar, Norway
Sverre Fehn, 1967–1979
The building's route along a concrete pathway passes through a glass wall and door, creating an invisible threshold between inside and outside.

2. The Penguin Pool at London Zoo, London, UK
Lubetkin Drake & Tecton, 1934
This pool design uses a ramp constructed from reinforced concrete, which creates a striking sculptural element linking two levels. It exploits the potential of concrete, demonstrating both structural and dynamic qualities.

3. The Barcelona Pavilion (exterior), constructed for the International Exposition in Barcelona of 1929
Ludwig Mies van der Rohe, 1928–1929
The pavilion's structure consisted of eight steel posts supporting a flat roof, with curtain glass walling and a handful of partition walls. The overall impression is of perpendicular planes in three dimensions forming a cool, luxurious space. The pavilion was demolished at the end of the exhibition, but a copy has since been built on the same site.

3

1. Le Modulor
© FLC / DACS, 2011, ProLitteris, Zurich
Le Corbusier, 1945

Le Corbusier explicitly used the golden ratio (see page 123) in his modular system for the scale of architectural proportion. He saw this system as a continuation of the long tradition of Vitruvius, Leonardo da Vinci's Vitruvian Man, the work of Leon Battista Alberti, and others who used the proportions of the human body to improve the appearance and function of architecture. In addition to the golden ratio, Le Corbusier based his system on human measurements, Fibonacci numbers (see page 123), and the double unit. He took da Vinci's suggestion of the golden ratio in human proportions to an extreme: he sectioned his model human body's height at the navel with the two sections in golden ratio, then subdivided those sections in golden ratio at the knees and throat; he used these golden ratio proportions in the modular system.

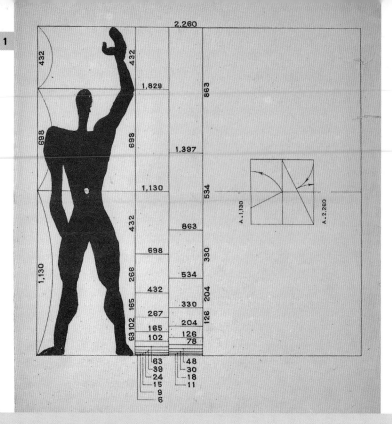

54 PURISM

During the modernist period, Swiss architect Le Corbusier (born Charles-Edouard Jeanneret) established principles of architecture that responded to Renaissance ideas and dogma. These governing rules were less about determining the form and more about establishing a direction for an architectural response.

Another important development for Le Corbusier was the modular system that, following the tradition of Leonardo da Vinci and Leon Battista Alberti amongst others, suggested that architecture needs to be centred around the proportions of the human body. The concept of *Le Modulor* created a measuring system that used human anthropometric dimensions as a way of determining form and space, and this system informed and underpinned the design of Le Corbusier's furniture, buildings and spaces.

Characteristics of modernist architecture

1. Pilotis: these are columns elevating the mass of the building off the ground.
2. The free plan: this is achieved through the separation of the load-bearing columns from the walls subdividing the space.
3. The free façade: this is the result of the free plan in the vertical plane.
4. The long, horizontal ribbon window.
5. The roof garden: this restores the area of ground covered by the structure.

2. The Schröder House, Utrecht, The Netherlands
Gerrit Rietveld, 1924–1925

The Schröder House is a kind of three-dimensional puzzle; it takes space and connects it both vertically and horizontally, using colour to signify the vertical and horizontal planes. The interior walls move to reveal larger open spaces. Everything is reinvented inside the house, all processes of living have been observed and responded to. The bathroom needs to be discovered and is unveiled in a cupboard. Sleeping, sitting and living are interweaved in one space. It is an experiment of space, form and function.

DE STIJL

In the twentieth century, the Dutch artistic movement, De Stijl (the style) began to connect the ideas of artists such as **Theo van Doesburg** to the notion of physical space. In the *De Stijl* journal van Doesburg explored the notion of space in relation to surface and colour. Similarly, Gerrit Rietveld developed ideas of space, form and colour in the design of his furniture and architecture.

Proponents of De Stijl sought to express a new utopian ideal of spiritual harmony and order. They advocated pure abstraction and universality by a reduction to the essentials of form and colour. They simplified visual compositions to the vertical and horizontal directions, and used only primary colours along with black and white.

Theo van Doesburg 1883–1931

Theo van Doesburg was one the founders of the De Stijl (the style) movement, which was concerned primarily with ideas of art and architecture. Interested in the abstraction of colour and form, De Stijl employed a visual code that connected colour and plane. Primary colours and black and white were used in both art and architecture to explore space and form.

Reconstructing a museum

Project: Neues Museum, Museum Island, Berlin

Architect: David Chipperfield Architects

Client: Stiftung Preussischer Kulturbesitz represented by Bundesamt für Bauwesen und Raumordnung

Location/date: Museum Island, Berlin, Germany / 1997–2009

This chapter is concerned with the idea of history and precedent and how this informs an architectural idea or project. This scheme by David Chipperfield Architects for the Neues Museum, Berlin is part of a complex of buildings known as Museum Island. All these buildings were built between 1840 and 1859. The site was semi-derelict for many years after it was damaged in the Second World War.

Responding to such a site with a contemporary architectural project requires careful reading and interpretation of the site, to ensure that the proposal does not compromise its historic integrity or identity.

The brief for the project was to reconstruct the original volume of the site, reinstating the original sequence of rooms and spaces. However, it was also important that the new interventions should be clearly distinct from the existing features, with no attempt to disguise the new elements as being part of the original structure.

1

RE-ESTABLISHMENT OF FORM + FIGURE

4

1. West façade of the Neues Museum.
2. Section through the staircase hall.
3. Concept sketch by David Chipperfield.
4. Floor plan level 1
The floor plan level shows the main entrance floor and courtyards.
Black denotes existing fabric, grey denotes new additions.

Before the project began, an archaeological investigation was necessary to record important aspects and features of the original building. The new spaces for the exhibition rooms were built from large prefabricated concrete elements, made from white cement mixed with white marble chips. The new staircase repeats the original without replicating it: it can be seen as distinctly different from the original; it is part of the language of the new architecture, the contemporary insertion.

There are areas within the building that have been reserved and are part of the interpretation of the space, allowing a sense of contact between the old and the new, including sections of wall that are exposed and colonnades that connect through the building.

The brief was to effect a restoration whilst preserving the physical character of the original building, which was largely made from stone. The restoration still leaves evident remnants from the building's history, and traces of war damage, including bullet holes, are still part of the visual history.

The building opened in 2009 and exhibits collections of the Egyptian museum and the Museum of Pre- and Early History.

3. & 4. Staircase hall
The new staircase (made from large format prefabricated concrete elements with marble aggregate) repeats the original without replicating it, and sits within a majestic hall that is preserved only as a brick volume, devoid of its original ornamentation.

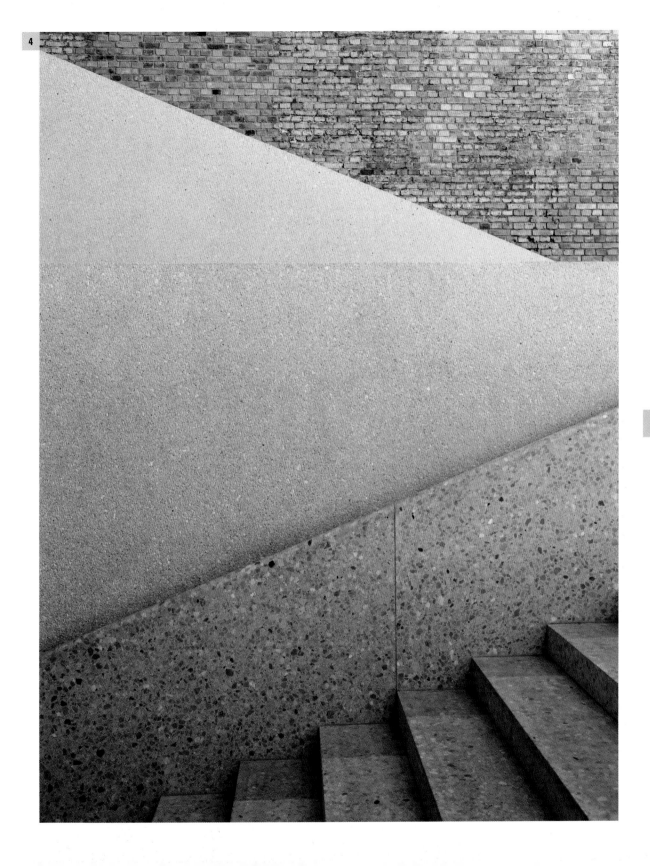

Exercise: Skylines

The history of a city can be seen on many levels; it is revealed by a panoramic view. It comprises buildings of many periods and historically can represent several centuries of development. The skyline of a city suggests change in structure, function and places expressed through changes in material as well as form.

To try to understand this skyline, which is part of the identity of a city, analysis of the city and its buildings can be a useful way to understand the historic development of a place.

For this exercise:

1. Take an image of a city skyline. This can be one photograph taken from a vantage point overlooking the city or it could be comprised of a series of images stitched together using software such as Adobe Photoshop.

2. To understand the form of the buildings individually, trace buildings of historical importance over the image.

3. Highlight and label these buildings. Discover as much as you can about the buildings, look online at local museums and libraries for information.

4. Once the city landscape has been described as a 'horizon', it may be useful to then investigate the buildings individually, in terms of material, and also to investigate historic maps to understand how the city has developed over a period of time.

Try to choose a mixture of new and old buildings and colour code them according to age. This will help you identify the historical morphology of your chosen city.

1. The Barcelona skyline
This photo of Barcelona shows a panoramic view of the city and the sketches overlaid highlight important elements in the skyline.

exercise

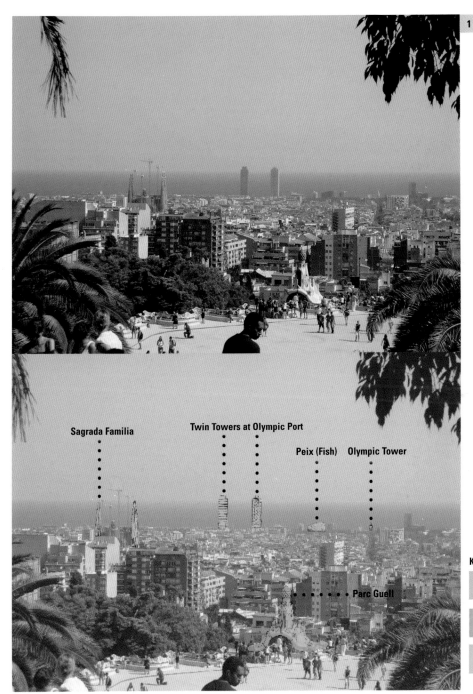

Sagrada Familia

Twin Towers at Olympic Port

Peix (Fish)   Olympic Tower

Parc Guell

Key

Pre-20th century

1900–1990

1950–2000

62

Construction is about the making of architecture; its physicality and its materiality. A building can be considered at a macro level, as a structural frame with a roof, walls and floors, but it simultaneously needs to be considered as a series of details that explain how the architectural components are combined and unified. For example, a building must operate and function effectively with design systems such as ventilation, heating or lighting, which provide variable and comfortable internal environments. Essentially, a building is a kind of machine; a series of interdependent parts and systems that collectively enable it to be effective and habitable.

1. Casa Milà (La Pedrera), Barcelona, Spain
Antoni Gaudí, 1912
Gaudí's design for the Casa Milà took into account the extreme heat of the Barcelona summers. He developed ventilation towers to take fresh air from the roof right down into the living areas of the building. Gaudí integrated innovative construction techniques and an empathy with the available materials, to create a sculptural and practical solution to a simple problem.

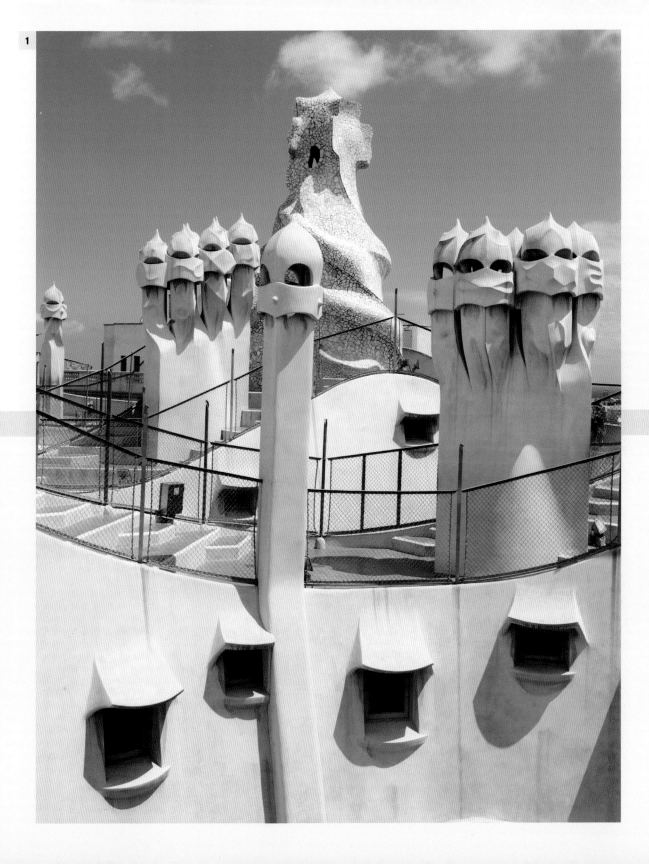

Materials

Construction techniques and systems are many and varied, but each is informed by the materials that are used.

This section will serve as an introduction to the typical materials used in construction, and will demonstrate how each can be used to provide a texture, form and spatial definition to a building.

Construction

MASONRY

Masonry is typified by constructions made from materials of the earth, such as brick and stone. When used in construction, masonry is a material that is stacked; traditionally heavier elements are placed on the lower layers and lighter layers are used as one moves vertically from the foundations to the roof. Some masonry construction is modular and as such it needs to behave in a particular way. For example, when openings are created in a brick wall, it is necessary to support the brickwork above. Typically voussoirs (a wedge-shaped or tapered brick or stone) are used to produce arches in a masonry wall, which provides the required support. Understanding the properties of masonry is an important part of understanding the architecture that uses it. For example, bricks must be stacked alternately, because if the courses are not varied the wall will be unstable and collapse.

The effect of a brick wall will vary according to the coursing patterns and brick colours available. Practically, a brick wall needs additional support over a certain height or it will not be stable, also it needs substantial support in its foundation to provide stability. Such concerns will ultimately inform the architectural design and its aesthetic expression.

1. Stone façade
This façade has been built from stone and comprises massive classical elements and more intricate carved detail.

2. Brick House, London, UK
Caruso St John, 2005
The floors and walls of this house are built of brick, inside and out. The use of one material binds the whole building. The arrangement of bricks within the mortar shifts as surfaces stretch, bend and twist, making them appear elastic and dynamic.

66 CONCRETE

Concrete is made of aggregate, gravel, cement, sand and water. It is the variable proportional quantities of these materials that give concrete its intrinsic strength.

Concrete can be brutal when used in large, heavy structures, but it can also have a subtlety to it, a quality that is exploited by Japanese architect **Tadao Ando**. In his architecture the shuttering, which supports the concrete while it is setting, is used to provide texture to the finished building. The memory of the shuttering's timber grain and the fixing bolts for the concrete's mould or formwork remain on the wall finish, giving the walls a depth and a sense of surface.

Sometimes, concrete is reinforced with a steel mesh to provide greater strength and stability. Reinforced concrete can span large distances and is used in engineering projects such as road building and bridge construction. Reinforced concrete allows enormous flexibility with large-scale structures.

The use of reinforced concrete was pioneered by French architect Auguste Perret. At the beginning of the twentieth century, Perret first worked alongside Le Corbusier and Peter Behrens, the German exponent of 'industrial design'. Behrens admired the engineer's ethic of mass production, logical design and function over style. Le Corbusier brought together the material and stylistic influences of Perret and Behrens in his 'Maison Dom-ino' plan of 1915 (see pages 72–73). This house would be made of reinforced concrete and was intended for mass production, but was also flexible: none of the walls were load-bearing and so the interior could be arranged as the occupant wished. Le Corbusier's radical ideas were given expression in his 1923 book *Vers Une Architecture* (*Towards a New Architecture*). 'A house', Le Corbusier intoned from its pages, 'is a machine for living in'.

Tadao Ando b. 1941

Ando is heavily influenced by the Japanese sense of materiality in construction. Light and space are important aspects of his work. Ando is most famously renowned for his use of concrete and application of simple geometry to plan, section and elevation.

Ando favours the use of timber shuttering, which he uses to create the 'mould' or formwork for in situ concrete (concrete poured on-site). When the shuttering is removed, the pattern of the timber and the bolts that connected it are still left on the concrete. This surface effect is a distinctive aspect of his work.

1. Saint Joseph Church, Le Havre, Normandy, France
Auguste Perret, 1957

Auguste Perret was one of the pioneers of reinforced concrete and he used it to beautiful effect in this 110 metre (361 feet) octagonal lantern-tower. The tower incorporates 6500 pieces of coloured glass, which light up the concrete and change colour depending on the position of the sun. The tower was designed by Auguste Perret and completed after his death by the architects of his studio.

2. Kidosaki House, Tokyo, Japan
Tadao Ando, 1982–1986

This house displays Ando's signature technique of building with concrete and the incorporation of the aesthetic produced from using timber shuttering. The holes in the walls indicate the position of the bolts that were used to hold together the shuttering.

Construction

68   GABION AND DRY-STONE WALLS

Gabion walls are retaining walls that are used to hold back earthworks or in the remodelling of landscapes for road construction or sea defences. A gabion wall is essentially a steel cage filled with large-grade stones. They are very easy to construct on difficult sites, and produce a quick-to-assemble and natural wall. Gabion walls have often been used as a form of architectural cladding to give a particular aesthetic to a building.

Dry-stone walls are constructed from found materials. Traditionally used to define boundaries, they are a precursor to gabion walls. Dry-stone walls require little skill to build and as the materials used to construct them are found on-site, there are no transportation methods to consider. These walls can be easily maintained too.

1. & 2. Gabion wall
A sketch of a gabion wall suggests the texture of the natural stone contrasted against the wire cage. The detail drawing illustrates how it is constructed.

3. The Gridshell, Weald and Downland Museum, West Sussex, UK
Edward Cullinan Architects, 1996–2002
This is an example of a grid shell timber frame. The main structure is made of oak laths (strips of timber) connected in a grid pattern that was then gradually lowered and bent into place. This has then been covered in timber tiles.

4. Traditional Japanese timber-frame house
This traditional Japanese house uses timber as the structural frame of the building. The timber frame raises the structure off the ground. The roof structure overhangs the main building, protecting it from sunlight and rain. In this example, the architect's choice of materials has responded directly to the local site conditions.

Timber can be used both as an exterior frame and as an interior finish. Some building types use timber for the structure or frame, the floor finish and the wall finish inside and out. Buildings constructed of timber were originally part of local traditions. A log cabin was built from the trees of the surrounding forest, it needed little transportation and assembly on site was quick.

Tradesmen who work with timber are carpenters if they deal with larger structural pieces of timber, or joiners if they make the finished elements for the interior such as stairs or doors. The more detailed furnishing elements are made by cabinetmakers.

Timber-framed buildings are usually of a limited scale; their limitation is caused by the size of the available material. Timber is cut to standard sizes and these work with other prefabricated components of the construction industry (such as doors and windows), and allow easy transportation and handling on-site.

Timber comes in various forms, it can be rough and textured or planed and finished, the choice will depend on where and how it is to be used. Timber is ultimately a flexible and natural material; it is light and easily adaptable on site and its natural colour and texture provide a range of finishes. When using timber, an important consideration for the architect is to ensure that the wood is sustainably sourced and responsibly harvested.

4

IRON AND STEEL

Iron and steel (an iron alloy mixed with carbon and other elements) can be used to construct the light frames that support a building, or to clad a building, providing a metal finish that can be both distinctive and durable.

Iron-frame buildings became popular during the period of nineteenth-century industrialization and structures such as London's Crystal Palace and the Eiffel Tower in Paris challenged the scale of structural possibility. Futuristic concepts, such as **Vladimir Tatlin's** tower, imagined an ambitious structure that would see the halls of state moving within a metal framework.

The concepts and constructions of the nineteenth century inspired many steel-framed buildings in the US and in Asia, which scaled previously unimagined heights. Important examples are the Chrysler Building in New York and the tallest building of the twentieth century, the Petronas Towers in Kuala Lumpur, which is 452 metres (1,483 feet).

Steel has liberated architectural form and has afforded the potential for a skyscraper scale of architecture. It is the ultimate flexible, durable and strong material. It can be manufactured off-site and individual elements can be bolted together. Materials such as these take architectural engineering expertise to its limits and enable the creation of impressive structures that can withstand the forces of nature.

**1. The Eiffel Tower, Paris, France
Gustave Eiffel, 1887–1889**
Designed as a temporary structure to celebrate the potential of engineering in France, the Eiffel Tower is made from iron using a number of prefabricated parts.

2. Reichstag dome, Berlin, Germany
Norman Foster, 1992–1999
The new Reichstag is a structure built on top of an original parliament building built in 1894.
The glass dome is supported within a steel frame, enabling views across Berlin.

GLASS

Glass is an exciting material because it has so many possibilities. It can appear as an invisible plane (due to its transparency), but it can also manipulate and filter light to create areas of shadow and light inside a building. Innovations in technology mean that glass can now be used structurally in certain applications to challenge our sense of space and surface.

The origins of glass lie in the Phoenician and Egyptian civilizations (circa 2500 BC, when it was used to produce decorative ceramics and jewellery) and the material is made by fusing the most basic natural materials: sand, soda (sodium carbonate) and lime. Glass has been used as a construction material since the eleventh century, when techniques were developed that enabled glass to be manufactured in sheets.

The use of glass has transformed the way buildings have been designed. It allows a definition between the inside and outside of a building, and defines a space with light. It has evolved to become a high-technology product.

Nowadays, for example, glass can self-clean if coated with titanium oxide, which absorbs ultra-violet rays and, through a chemical process, gradually and continuously breaks down any organic matter that builds up on the surface, which is then washed away by rainwater. Laminated glass can incorporate layers of coloured glass, which react to changes in temperature and so alter the mood inside a space. Similarly, 'smart' glass can vary the amount of heat and light passing through it using electro-chromic and liquid crystal technologies. Privalite glass allows an electrical current to turn transparent glass into an opaque screen by realigning electrons within the construction of the glass sheet, and Pilkington K glass separates the different types of radiation passing through it to prevent buildings from overheating.

Glass possesses the unique quality of allowing interior spaces to appear as though they are actually part of the outside, of nature, or part of a greater whole.

Elements

At its most basic level, there are four major elements in any building's construction: the structure (or framework), the foundations, the roof and the walls and openings. Once these elements are determined, the building will have a defined form, and only then can the more detailed design decisions be considered.

STRUCTURE

In this context, structure is concerned with how the building is supported, and this usually takes one of two forms: structures of solid construction (where the walls support the building) or structures of framework construction (where the frame is independent of the building's walls and floors).

As the name suggests, solid construction creates a heaviness and solidity to buildings and will define a building's interior spaces. It creates a permanent and massive sense of the architectural form. Solid construction can use masonry, which can be modules of natural stone or brick, or it may be achieved using concrete, either prefabricated (made off-site) or in situ (poured into moulds on-site).

Using a frame construction provides a great deal of flexibility in terms of the building's internal layout and the position of its openings (such as doors and windows). The structural frame can be made of many materials such as timber, steel or concrete, and it can be very quickly constructed and even adapted to suit future needs.

A classic example of a framework construction is Le Corbusier's conceptual Dom-ino frame. It is a concrete frame that connects the floor planes and the roof plane with a single staircase. Doing so allows the internal and external walls to be positioned so as to respond to the internal arrangement of the building. This structure led to the birth of the 'free plan'.

The free plan was a revolutionary concept because it proposed that the walls and openings were not dependent on a building's structure. Instead, a framework gave freedom to the internal layout of the plan and the position of its doors and windows. This concept is exemplified by Le Corbusier's Villa Savoye in Poitiers, north of Paris.

1. Musée du Quai Branly, Paris, France
Jean Nouvel, 2006

This museum is located alongside the River Seine in Paris, France. The museum is surrounded by a glazed screen that separates the garden space acoustically from the busy road, but maintains the visual connection to the Seine. The screen also enhances the idea that the garden serves as an introduction to the museum. It is also an independent structure that defines the museum's garden.

2. The Dom-ino frame

The title of Le Corbusier's theoretical study of a structural frame originates from the Latin for house: 'domus'. The Dom-ino frame was conceived as an affordable prefabricated system that would free interior and exterior walls from structural constraints.

1. Diagram of the Pyramide du Louvre's foundations
This diagram shows how the glazed structure of the Pyramide du Louvre is actually the tip of the building, which extends beneath the ground.

Construction

74 FOUNDATION

The structure of the building has to be supported at the point where it touches the ground; this support is usually referred to as the building's foundation. The foundation essentially supports the frame or walls of the structure and needs to be sufficiently strong to respond to the ground conditions around the building and any anticipated movement. Ground movement will be affected by local conditions such as the geology of the site, in particular, the dryness of the ground. Large structures or trees nearby could also affect the stability of the building. A structural engineer would normally advise on the type of foundations that would best respond to the building design and the site ground conditions.

There are many buildings that are built partially or wholly underground; this may be due to local topography, required functionality or restrictions of site development. In urban centres, where there is often pressure on land values, building underground can be a financially viable proposition.

In some climates, building underground can provide an extra dimension of protection from the environment. These types of subterranean building require specific construction methods; essentially a retaining wall (a wall that is holding back the soil or earth) is required to define the building's structure, and this needs to be both insulated and made to incorporate a waterproof layer to prevent water penetration from the surrounding ground.

2

**2. Pyramide du Louvre, Paris, France
I. M. Pei, 1989**
The Pyramide du Louvre was a later addition to the original museum. The structure above ground is an entrance portico to the museum's main galleries and an introduction to the subterranean spaces beneath. The glazed structure brings light into the museum spaces beneath ground.

3. Neue Nationalgalerie, Berlin, Germany
Ludwig Mies van der Rohe, 1968
The Neue Nationalgalerie (New National Gallery) is essentially a steel frame or pavilion with glass walls as simple planes dividing inside from outside.

WALLS AND OPENINGS

The wall is an architectural aspect that creates an enclosure, marking the definition between the interior and exterior boundaries. Walls can be load-bearing; supporting a roof or floor plane, or non-load-bearing; acting simply as a division of space.

Curtain walls are an example of external walls that are non-load-bearing, and are used to define inside space from outside space. They are waterproof and designed to cope with external dynamic pressures. Originally, curtain walls were made from steel, but are now more commonly made from a light metal frame that is infilled with glass, metals or veneers such as timber or stone.

Openings in walls allow light into the interior spaces, provide ventilation and also, critically, allow entry to and exit from a building or space. Any opening compromises the idea of enclosure and separates the internal climate from the external climate. For this reason, openings need to be considered very carefully and in great detail.

The door opening is often the most celebrated aspect of any elevation as it marks the point of entry and often defines a building's identity. Doorways are often marked by thresholds, which are raised steps or plinths that serve to further define the point of entry. Canopies or covering structures can also provide a sense of shelter at a doorway.

Windows tend to vary in size to reflect the range of activities that are likely to take place inside, and the kind of light, view and privacy expected by the building's occupants. Picture windows frame views across rural or urban landscapes to reduce the sense of separation between the inside and the outside.

76 ROOFS

The roof defines the top layer of a building; it offers protection and provides a sense of safety and security. A roof can be extensive, acting as a structure that is independent of the building or buildings that it covers, or it can be precisely related to the building outline it covers.

The roof of a building is normally determined by its function, but the building's immediate context will also inform the roof's design. For example, if there are pitched roofs in the vicinity then this will probably create a precedent for a particular formal response.

Climate is also a determining factor. Rainfall needs to be quickly and efficiently drained away, which might dictate the necessity of a sloped roof. In very warm climates, a roof offers protection from the intense heat and overhanging roof structures can provide additional shelter to the streets below. In climates where snow is a consideration, the roof pitch is critical, in order to prevent snow settling on the roof surface.

1. Giant's Causeway competition proposal
David Mathias and Peter Williams, 2005
The roof can form a significant part of the architectural concept. This competition proposal for a visitor centre in Northern Ireland integrates the roof as a part of the surrounding landscape. The roof forms part of an extended journey that connects to the building idea.

2. Subway station at the Beijing Capital International Airport, Terminal 3, China
This glazed roof floods the space beneath with natural light, the structure gives a pattern to the ceiling that is reflected on the floor beneath. Terminal 3 was designed by a consortium of NACO (Netherlands Airport Consultants B.V), UK Architect Foster and Partners and ARUP. Lighting was designed by UK lighting architects Speirs and Major Associates.

Prefabrication

Prefabricated constructions describe those buildings whose parts or components have been specifically manufactured to enable easy assembly on site. Prefabricated components can range from a small factory-made element such as a chair, to larger construction elements such as pre-cast concrete slabs, and even whole housing units that are installed and assembled on-site. Prefabricated elements can be partially assembled off-site and then finished on-site, or be supplied fully finished and ready to use.

Richard Rogers' Lloyds Building in London (constructed 1979–1986) used prefabricated toilet units, which were hoisted into place and bolted onto the structure. This revelation saved enormous amounts of construction time and allowed units to be made in factory-controlled conditions, precisely and efficiently.

Prefabrication techniques have developed enormously since then. Huf Haus is a German company, one of many that provides buildings almost in kit form, as a series of prefabricated elements that arrive on site and are bolted together to produce a perfect factory-machined result. Whole blocks of housing have been produced in this way; units are first fitted out and then transported to site and slotted into preformed structures.

Prefabrication brings many advantages including speed of construction and assembly, strict quality control (all elements are made in factories where there are fewer variables than on a building site) and the production of adaptable, light and mobile structures; their flexible quality means they can be dismantled and erected elsewhere.

1

1. London prefabricated housing scheme
Individual prefabricated elements such as bathroom units can be dropped into place during construction. These elements could be as big as a whole housing unit. The limitations are transportation and installation factors.

2. Prefabricated habitat housing student sketch
This sketch shows an experimental housing block that was built in 1967 for the World's Fair in Montreal. It demonstrates the concept of stacking prefabricated units to create an apartment block or settlement.

3. Prefabricated architecture student scheme
This image indicates how a housing scheme could be developed with different prefabricated elements, each one dropped in at a different stage of the project's lifespan.

3

Structure

Our cities offer numerous possibilities to reinvent structures or forms that are part of their skyline or architectural heritage, and which have been made redundant through changing uses of spaces and places. Reinvention is an opportunity that architects can respond to positively. Doing so requires sensitive and careful consideration of the history of the site, in particular how an existing building can adapt to new functions without compromising important aspects of its character and form.

Reinventing existing buildings through design is often a more sustainable way to deal with the structure, as it will incorporate existing forms and materials.

A good example of this is the Tate Modern gallery in London. Now an extremely successful gallery, the building was a redundant power station that was reinvented by Swiss architects Herzog and de Meuron in 2000.

The Tate Modern has since become one of the most famous art galleries in the world. The design used the impact and scale of the existing building to great effect. It acts as a beacon, responding to the building's site on the south bank of the River Thames in London. Other elements, such as a bridge and a riverside walk, created the urban infrastructure that makes the gallery now a central part of its surrounding location.

1. The Great Court at the British Museum, London, UK
Foster + Partners, 1994–2000
The Great Court was originally an underused external courtyard that was reinvented by **Foster + Partners** in 1994. The area was covered with a unique glazed structure to become a vibrant internal courtyard serving as café, reception and information spaces for the museum.

2. The Tate Modern, London, UK
Herzog and de Meuron 1998–2000
The construction of the Tate Modern formed part of the redevelopment of London's South Bank. This former power station was redefined; its external form was already powerful and iconic – the internal spaces, such as the turbine hall, were industrial in scale – and this was used to dramatic effect in the gallery's central exhibition space, allowing large-scale exhibits and events to be staged.

Foster + Partners

Norman Foster's practice is concerned with 'hi-tech' architecture that uses modern technology and intelligent materials. Foster + Partners has been involved in projects ranging from product and building design to refurbishment and urban master planning. Innovative use of glass has always been a feature of its work.

Recent projects include the Great Court at the British Museum, the Hong Kong and Shanghai Bank, the Reichstag redesign and the international airport terminal in Beijing.

2

Innovation

Designing buildings raises many issues concerning sustainability. At a macro level, the design of a city for example, there are issues of transportation, energy efficiency or carbon emissions to resolve; at the micro level the design of individual buildings, the types of materials used and how they are manufactured and sourced are important considerations in sustainable architectural design.

Sustainability is a very broad term when applied to architecture and refers to the nature of the construction, the materials used and their origins. For example, does a timber specified for a particular project come from a sustainable resource? Is it from a managed forest where each tree removed is replaced by another tree, or is it from a hardwood forest, where the removal of trees is causing irreparable damage to the area and ultimately the planet?

There are also broader issues to consider in the context of sustainability. For example, how far do the materials that are used in a building travel to get to the site? If slate from China is used in a building in Europe, the financial cost may be less than locally sourced materials, but the carbon cost in terms of fuel used to transport these materials is significant. The carbon footprint of a building is the amount of carbon expended to make the materials and transport those materials to the site. Whenever materials are sourced or specified, these considerations should be taken into account.

Another consideration is the energy efficiency of the building over its lifetime. Insulation, for example, is essential to reduce the amount of fuel needed to maintain the building at a comfortable ambient temperature. Is the energy used to power the building renewable? How are waste products treated and disposed of? All such questions of sustainability need to be considered as the building design develops.

When choosing a site, important infrastructure issues should also be considered, such as public transport links to minimize unnecessary travel and fuel costs.

1. BedZED Eco-community Development, Surrey, UK
Bill Dunster Architects, 2002
Beddington Zero Energy Development (BedZED) is the UK's largest
zero energy development. It has housing and work spaces that are
designed specifically as an approach to sustainable living in the
city. The development uses energy from renewable resources and
includes solar energy systems and waste-water recycling.

Innovative materials

Advances in material technologies present new opportunities for contemporary architecture. Material innovations from design areas such as fashion and product design can also inform building design. These innovations can stimulate a new way of thinking about building, they may make the construction process easier or cheaper or create some visual statement.

Interactive technologies provide the potential for buildings to respond to user activities. Movement sensors in and around buildings allow services such as lighting and ventilation to operate remotely. Materials can also react to movement or light through thermal sensors, and wireless technologies allow much greater flexibility in the way we use buildings.

Combining materials can increase a material's flexibility and application opportunities. Composite glass flooring, for example, which is made from structural glass and aluminium, combines the lightness and strength of aluminium with the transparency of glass to create large glass panels that can also be used as floor panels because they are weight-bearing.

Translucent or transparent concrete, which is made from glass and polymerized synthetics, has revolutionized the properties of concrete. As well as great flexibility (it can be poured and moulded), it has the added benefit of allowing light to pass through it. Structural columns using this material become visibly lighter as a result.

The increased demand for energy efficiency in buildings, and the potential to make surfaces a source of harnessing energy, has meant that the solar panel has become more prevalent and more flexible in its application. Solar panels can now be an integrated part of a roof system, rather than treated as a bolt-on element, and this presents the architect with increased design opportunities.

Innovation can also mean using materials in a new context. Reflective materials, traditionally used in aerospace design, are now being used in roofing insulation. Sheep's wool is often used in building insulation as it has a high thermal value. Straw bales, once a localized building material, are now viewed as a sustainable material for many different contexts.

The future of construction materials and technology is interwoven with the development of 'smart' materials from a variety of industries. Ascertaining how these technologies and innovations can be incorporated into building materials and strategies, to make living and working a more dynamic and interactive experience, is the challenge facing architects today.

1. The Libeskind Building of the Jewish Museum Berlin (Jüdisches Museum Berlin), Germany
Studio Daniel Libeskind, 1999
The Libeskind Building in the Jewish Museum Berlin uses a distinctive cladding material, zinc, which contrasts with the heavy stone buildings that surround it. The material will also change colour and texture over time as it is exposed to the climate, adapting to its surroundings.

2. Structural glass
The transparency of this staircase allows the light to flow down through the building, providing a visual as well as physical link between the floors.

Designing a pavilion

Project: UAE Pavilion, Shanghai Expo 2010

Architect: Foster + Partners

Client: UAE National Media Council

Location / date: Shanghai, China / 2008–2010

There are many innovative systems used in building construction that challenge contemporary ideas about architecture and form. Using new structural systems can suggest a new set of architectural forms that are sculptural; that challenge preconceptions about 'buildings'. Foster + Partners has a reputation for architectural innovation: sometimes the structural solution can drive the aesthetic of a project. A pavilion structure is an opportunity to showcase new ideas and challenge architectural convention.

The UAE pavilion was a temporary structure designed and constructed for the 2010 Shanghai Expo. It was designed to showcase innovation in the United Arab Emirates (UAE) in response to the 'Better Cities, Better Lives' theme of the exposition. For example, one of the projects being showcased in the building is the Masdar masterplan project for a new carbon-neutral community in Abu Dhabi.

The brief was to accommodate 450 people and create 3000 square metres (32,300 square feet) of exhibition space. The structure requires a space that can be flexible in terms of exhibition and display space. The concept for the scheme developed from a response to a local landscape feature: the sand dune.

The concept suggests a sand dune in terms of its form, through its soft profile. Also the surface of the pavilion is smooth on the side that is exposed to the wind and has a rougher texture on the other side. The north- and south-facing elevations also contrast with one another. The north elevation is more open, to allow natural light to filter into the space within; the south-facing elevation is more solid, to attempt to minimize solar gain.

The structure of the pavilion is comprised of a lattice of flat stainless steel panels. They have been designed with a fixing system so that they can be easily attached and separated to allow the pavilion to be assembled and taken apart quickly. The internal fit-out is by Ralph Applebaum Associates, and the lighting focuses onto the exposed roof structure to illuminate the structural concept from within.

1. Elevation and section drawings
Elevations and sections through the main structure.

1. Exterior skin
The exterior skin of the roof reflects light.

2. Pavilion entrance
The entrance relates to the large public square outside.

1

Construction

2

3. Exhibition space
The interior with large exhibition objects freestanding in the space.

4. Open plan space
The interior space is a large open-plan area with enough room for projection and interactive display.

Exercise: Axonometric drawing

An axonometric drawing allows for a three-dimensional overview of a scheme. It is essentially a plan extruded upwards, almost giving the impression of looking at a model of a building from above. Exploded axonometrics are three-dimensional drawings that have been separated into a series of layers to explain an architectural idea.

For this exercise, take the plan of a building and draw it in axonometric projection. To create an exploded axonometric drawing, think about the layers within the building.

In the example drawing of the Barcelona Pavilion, the structural columns are shown on the plan and elements such as solid walls, glass walls and the roof have been identified on separate layers. You can add as little or as much detail as necessary and it can be helpful to use colours to pick out key materials. Materials can also be identified by linking photographs to selected areas.

1. The Barcelona Pavilion (sketch), constructed for the International Exposition in Barcelona of 1929
Ludwig Mies van der Rohe, 1928-1929
This three-dimensional drawing of the Barcelona Pavilion, designed by Mies van der Rohe, explains the building as a series of horizontal and vertical planes with structural elements supporting the roof.

Construction

exercise

Chapter 4
Representation

In this context, representation refers to the range of methods that can be used to communicate architectural ideas and concepts. Some of these techniques are traditionally associated with architectural expression (such as plan, section, and elevation drawings), and others are borrowed or adapted from other disciplines, such as storyboarding from film production, computer-generated imagery from areas of digital media, or freehand sketching and analytical drawing techniques that are most commonly associated with artistic techniques.

1. Section drawing
This student drawing describes the spaces in a building; the use of figures suggests a story of how the building will be used. The use of shadow offers a suggestion of the quality of the living spaces within.

CAD drawing

Over the last 20 years, technological advances have presented a range of new possibilities for architects. All students now learn some form of computer-aided design (CAD) skills at schools of architecture and it is now an accepted language in the discourse of the discipline.

This technological advance has presented a whole new interface to describe architectural spaces and has allowed new sorts of architectural forms to evolve.

FACILITATING OR LIMITING?

At one level, CAD provides an exploratory design tool; different software packages, used independently or collectively, allow for new initiatives and forms of expression. CAD also allows for quick translation of ideas because plan and section drawings can be easily adapted and developed. CAD can also be used to produce a series of related images, each one providing an additional layer of information. Collectively, the series will form a 'package' of information that will better communicate the concept or construction instructions.

Sometimes, however, the computer can be seen as a limiting factor. The CAD image renders as a graphic, which can be seductive and impressive, but it's still the architecture as built, inhabitable space, that needs to be tested and read as a believable three-dimensional form.

There are interesting interfaces in the use of CAD; some of the expressions of the buildings can appear surreal, while other interpretations can sometimes appear so real and so perfect in their imagery, that one is forced to ask whether the representation is a photograph of reality or a computer-generated model.

1. CAD drawing
This CAD drawing is developed using Adobe Photoshop software to overlay different images and information to suggest how this urban space may be designed.

2. & 3. CAD photomontage
This set of images uses a combination of site photos and CAD models to describe a design idea.

PHOTOMONTAGE

A very effective mechanism in CAD drawing is the photomontage technique. It produces a seductive image that is often used as a means to convince or demonstrate that the architecture can 'fit' any proposed client requirements or is appropriate for its intended site. Photomontage images are frequently described as artist impressions because they often mix digital photographs of an existing site with computer-generated models. Photomontage images are essentially 'stage managed' by the designer to obtain the best view or the most impressive angle of the proposed idea. The underlying aim of any representation technique will be to display the concept at its best.

2

3

Sketching
Architectural drawing tends to fall into one of three broad categories: conceptual, developmental and realization. The sketch drawing can exist across all categories, but it is used most readily at the conceptual stage because it is the quickest and simplest way to explain complex ideas in architecture.

96

Representation

Sketches can be quick and inspired or more detailed and produced to scale. There are even software packages available that attempt to recreate the loose dynamic aspect of sketching (such as Google SketchUp). There is power in a sketch; it is a personal and immediate connection between the idea and the rendering of a two-dimensional representation on paper. A sketch has character and it lacks precision, which is its attraction. In the sleight of the hand, the thickness of the pencil line, all sorts of issues can be implied and hidden. Sketching happens at all stages of the design process, but in particular at the start of it, when the detail hasn't yet been considered, allowing the potential for anything to happen.

a mindscape: october in denmark

1

SITE 4

SITE 6

LINEAR
AXIS

THE IDEA IS KEY

Anyone can sketch; it's easy to manipulate lines on paper. The importance is the sophistication of the idea behind the line and the thinking that stimulates it. Accuracy or even technical skill aren't the primary considerations here, it's the idea. Leonardo da Vinci, for example, used sketches to analyse the human body, to better understand the mechanics of muscles and the structure of the skeleton. He used his sketches to inform his subsequent designs of machines and architecture.

The sketch is a loose drawing, and as such it can be reworked and redirected to explore different possibilities. A sketch can be of a fantastically impossible idea, something futuristic or surreal, or it can outline the details of a concept and how these are applied to a piece of architecture. Sketching allows the exploration of an idea, a testing of possibilities. Only when the idea exists on paper in sketch form, can it be further developed.

3

CONCEPTUAL SKETCHES

Conceptual sketches are created the moment that an
architectural idea is conceived. These sketches connect
idea with architecture. They can be abstract, metaphorical
or even a formalized doodle that allows the journey of
thinking to develop.

Representation

Peter Zumthor b. 1943
Peter Zumthor is a Swiss architect who has a reputation for his
sensitivity to context and materiality. He is a writer as well as
an architect and is particularly interested to describe his
buildings poetically and philosophically in terms of material,
light and space. Some of his seminal pieces have been cultural
buildings including galleries, museums and places of worship.

1. & 2. Serpentine Gallery Pavilion
Peter Zumthor, 2011
The Serpentine Gallery is a temporary structure that was placed in
Hyde Park, London as a summer pavilion, and is part of a series of
structures by renowned architects. Zumthor was interested in the
relationship between the garden and the pavilion. The hard exterior
contrasts with the Japanese-inspired garden within.

3. & 4. Analytical sketches
Analytical sketches deconstruct an idea in order to allow a better understanding of the development and assembly behind it. Both of these analytical sketches investigate ideas of stairs and spaces.

ANALYTICAL SKETCHES

Analytical sketches take an idea and examine it in detail, usually as part of a series of steps to explain why something is the way it is, or how it will eventually be. Analytical sketches allow the deconstruction of an idea. Spaces can be analysed in terms of the activities or functions that will occur within them and cities can be analysed in terms of the experiences, journeys or building mass they contain.

Buildings can be specifically analysed in terms of measurables such as the amount of light in, or the function of, its different rooms and spaces. Such analysis is central to understanding the present condition, so that it can be responded to through the architectural idea or proposition. This analysis needs to be concise and diagrammatically clear.

CAD drawing < **Sketching** > Scale

OBSERVATIONAL SKETCHES

Some of the best ideas come from acquiring a better understanding of something that already exists. Observational sketches can reveal details of form and structure that help provide better understanding. This type of sketching can be likened to life drawing; by drawing the body the artist develops a greater understanding of it, both proportionally and mechanically. The same process can be applied to drawing a building; doing so allows the exploration of its individual components and an awareness of how they relate to the whole. For example, the details of how different materials are juxtaposed and joined together can reveal expressive or implicit architectural ideas.

1. & 2. Student sketches
These sketches are careful studies of buildings both inside and outside. Care has been taken to study and draw detail, with effective use of colour and texture to intensify the image.

3. Saint Benedict Chapel, Graubünden, Switzerland
Peter Zumthor, 1987–1989
Daylight entering the interior space of the chapel. Compare this to the sketches shown on page 101.

SKETCHBOOKS: IDEA COLLECTIONS

Sketchbooks represent a collection of ideas and different journeys of exploration and understanding. They are emotional, raw and bursting with potential. An architect's sketchbook allows an idea to be taken and pursued beyond reality, sometimes in the wrong direction, until there is no mileage left in it. At other times it explores concepts that start as two-dimensional, raw sketches and finish as a realized building; the leap of ambition can be enormous!

Sketchbooks contain visual notes to stimulate and inform. This form of note-taking is developed through observation of real situations (understanding how buildings are) as well as theoretical explorations (why buildings are).

The process of developing an architectural idea can be well documented and recorded in a sketchbook, but this works in conjunction with the computer in the communication of architectural design. What starts as a concept sketch is then drawn to scale on a computer. Parts of this drawing can then be further analysed and redesigned in the sketchbook, before being developed as a finished proposal on the computer. The computer and the sketchbook represent the two diverse types of thinking that are needed for architecture; the sketchbook is imaginative and intuitive, and the computer defined and precise.

4. & 5. Perspective sketches
These drawings explore the way in which light enters Saint Benedict's Chapel. The use of colour on these perspective sketches creates an animated and realistic impression of the internal space.

CAD drawing < **Sketching** > Scale

Scale

Scale is a critical consideration in architectural and spatial design as it allows the comparison of a drawing or model of an architectural idea to its real-size representation. Scale is the relative representation of an idea to a measurement, or system of measurement, that is universally known or understood.

Understanding a scale system allows the idea of a specific space to be properly communicated. Aligning the idea to something that we understand the scale of will help us to better understand the proportions of a concept. For example, a person placed in a room or building is something we can immediately connect with in terms of scale. Similarly, a piece of furniture, such as a bed or chair, also relates to human scale and so again its placement within a room will help our understanding of architectural concepts, proportions and spaces.

Scale is one of the first notions we need to understand in order to start designing structures for people to inhabit, because it allows us to comprehend how we can physically occupy a space – whether it is intended to be a tight, intimate and close space, or a loose, large and open one.

The Powers of Ten

Scale needs to be understood in both a physical and a relative sense. *The Powers of Ten* (1968), a film by Charles and Ray Eames, is an important study of scale. This film opens with a shot of a person lying on a picnic mat. The viewer can easily comprehend the recognizable scale of this as it is full-size or 1:1 ratio. The film then moves each frame by a power of ten, first to 1:10 (one tenth real size), and then 1:100 (one hundredth real size) and so on until the scale reaches the (then) knowledge of the universe.

This film provides a useful way to understand the relative nature of scale. Understanding scale necessitates an understanding of the actual or real size of objects as well as the perceived and represented size of objects. Scale is a concept of imagining spaces, objects or buildings at different levels of detail.

For more information visit www.powersof10.com

1. Scale models (shown left to right: 1:2000, 1:200 and 1:20)
These models are produced at a range of scales, each is increasing in scale by a factor of 10. Each incremental increase in scale allows more detail to be understood.

Scale Ratio	Application
1:1 Full size	Details of furniture and materials
1:2	Details of furniture and materials
1:5	Building and interior details
1:10	Building and interior details
1:20	Building and interior details
1:50	Interior details and small building plans
1:100	Overall larger building plans
1:200	Overall larger building plans and site layouts
1:500	Site layouts and context relationship
1:1000	Surrounding landscape and site location
1:1250	Map scale location
1:2500	Large map scale location

1

Scale of 1:2000

Scale of 1:200

Scale of 1:20

Sketching < **Scale** > Orthographic projection

APPROPRIATE SCALE

Representation

Appropriateness of scale, using the correct ratio to explain the information effectively, is crucial as it affects the communication and understanding of a concept. Architects use different scales than those used by engineers or other designers.

The first scale ratio to understand is 1:1, or full-size scale, which is real or actual size and is used in architecture for designing small components and conducting smaller investigations of space. Sometimes spaces can be mocked up at real scale, much like a stage set, to investigate a concept. All scale ratios are expressed proportionately to full-size scale.

After 1:1, each scale ratio is used in different contexts to allow varying aspects or details of an idea to be drawn and expressed.

Construction details are expressed as 1:5 or 1:10 scale, Such details are usually concerned with understanding junctions in buildings, for example, where walls meet the floor and the roof or the foundations.

The next range of scale, 1:20 and 1:50, are traditionally used to understand the interior aspects of rooms and layouts or to communicate a larger idea of construction and structure.

Building layouts are explored at 1:50, 1:100 and 1:200 depending on the size of the structure. Site relationships are drawn at scale ratios of 1:100, 1:200 and 1:500. The largest scale drawings are maps that indicate site location, and these are usually produced at ratios of 1:1000, 1:1250 or 1:2500.

1–5. Scale drawings

1. A detail drawing normally at 1:5 or 1:10 scale to show material connections.

2. A section 1:20 or 1:50 shows relationships between spaces.

3. A 1:50 or 1:100 scale drawing can be used for plan and section drawings of a whole building.

4. Drawings at 1:200 or 1:500 scale are used for a site location plan to explain immediate context.

5. A map scale 1:1250 or 1:2500 describes a much larger context of a city or landscape.

5

Sketching < **Scale** > Orthographic projection

Orthographic projection

Orthographic projection is a means of representing a three-dimensional object in two dimensions. In architecture, orthographic projection generally takes one of three forms: plan, section and elevation drawings.

A plan is an imagined horizontal cross section of a room or building approximately 1.2 metres (3.9 feet) above ground or finished floor level. A section drawing shows a vertical cross section of a building or space. The elevation drawing displays the building's face or façade.

PLANS

All these types of drawings are measured; they each use scale to communicate the spaces and forms contained within them. When architects refer to a 'full set' of drawings, this term encompasses plan, section, elevation and detail drawings. With the full set of information, and with each drawing type displayed at varying scales, a building design can be communicated clearly and understood as a three-dimensional proposition. It can be costed by a quantity surveyor, an engineer can see the architectural intention, and a builder can use the drawings to construct the building accurately. Independently, each type of drawing communicates specific information, but collectively they explain the architecture completely.

Plans need to explain the horizontal layers of the building; the basement (or below ground area), the ground floor, all other floor levels and the roof plan.

A site location plan is the first kind of drawing that explains a building. It is usually a bird's eye view and shows the surrounding area, incorporating the entrance to the building and, importantly, a north point.

Plans can be selective and just show a single room, or they can be diagrammatic and display the whole building. The amount of detail in a plan can vary enormously. It may have furniture within it to show the scale and use of a space, or show the materials intended to be used for the interior, or it can simply display spaces, walls, windows and doors. A plan drawing will contain as much (or as little) information as is available at each stage of the design process.

1. Eccleston House site location plan drawing
John Pardey Architects, 2006
The site plan of this house explains the relationship of the building
to its immediate context. The plan includes information about the
surrounding landscape, available parking, orientation and the
relationship of the house's rooms to external views and vistas. There
is a clarity about the plan of the building when it is viewed in the
context of its surrounding landscape.

1

1. Eccleston House elevation drawing
John Pardey Architects, 2006
Context is described in an elevation drawing as it shows the building
clearly in its environment. This elevation drawing gives us a sense
of scale, using figures and materials with shadow and colour. The
trees provide a sense of scale to the building in relation to its
surrounding landscape.

2. Eccleston House final presentation plan
John Pardey Architects, 2006
This layout drawing showing the building's elevations describes
the setting of the house in the context of its surroundings, a first floor
plan and a range of perspective images. This provides a complete
description of the scheme, from inside layout to the external form,
as well as its relationship to the site.

north elevation

01 chimney / barbecue
02 living
03 dining
04 kitchen
05 pool
06 entrance
07 study / play room
08 guest bedroom
09 utility / bathroom
10 day room
11 entrance court
12 enclosed garden
13 eucalyptus tree (existing)
14 existing garage
15 entrance void
16 bedroom
17 bathroom
18 ensuite bathroom
19 master bedroom
20 dressing area
21 brise soleil pagoda
22 sedum roof finish

a western red cedar cladding
b aluminium framed glazing ppc, colour 9007
c rendered wall, white / dark green
d oak joists
e exposed concrete slab
f rendered chimney / barbecue

first floor plan

existing entrance perspective

proposed entrance perspective

south elevation

title: Proposed first floor plan, north + south elevation   status: planning   drawing no: LCE - PP- 05   scale: 1:100   date: Oct 2005

project: Latchmore Corner   revision:

JOHN PARDEY ARCHITECTS
www.johnpardeyarchitects.com

1. Elevation drawing
This image of the proposed long elevation of Mottisfont Abbey in Romsey, UK, describes the building and its relationship to the landscape and woodland behind it.

2. Section drawing
A section drawing allows this church to be understood in its site context, revealing the double height spaces within.

3. Sketches
These sketches are not drawn to any scale, but they describe the design idea as a section, plan and perspective.

ELEVATIONS

Elevation drawings display a building's or structure's façade. Elevation drawings are usually created from the view of each direction that the building or site faces (the north-facing elevation or the west-facing elevation and so on). These drawings can provide a sense of depth by using tone to show where shadows may fall and in doing so affect the building or site. Elevation drawings are designed using mathematical precision, geometry and symmetry to determine the overall effect.

It is important to design and read an elevation drawing alongside a plan in order to understand how the elevation relates to the plan and to see the 'bigger picture'. For example, the position of a window is important in terms of how a room functions, but the window also has to relate to the whole elevation and its composition. It is necessary for the architect to understand spaces and buildings at different scales and levels. In this example, the window relates to the room at one level and then to the street elevation at another.

SECTIONS

A section drawing is an imagined 'slice' or cross section of a building or space. Section drawings impart an understanding of how spaces connect and interrelate with one another, and describe these relationships in a way that a plan can't. For example, relationships between different interior spaces and floor levels can be revealed, or the connection between the inside and outside of a building can be seen.

Perspective

Perspective drawings are very easily understood by those who may not be familiar with reading two-dimensional plans and section drawings. They are based on the idea of an individual's viewpoint (or perspective) and convey a 'real' impression or view of a space or place.

SKETCH PERSPECTIVE

To sketch in perspective is to try to create an impression of a 'real' view. To sketch in this way, the view first needs to be studied carefully and the point at which all the 'lines' of view appear to converge needs to be identified. This abstract point is called the vanishing point. This concept can be better understood by taking a photograph of a space and finding the point at which all the lines within it cross. This vanishing point is then used as a reference for the creation of perspective images.

Once the vanishing point is established, converging lines can be created to indicate the edges of surrounding elements, or in a room to distinguish horizontal planes (such as walls) from vertical planes (such as floors and ceilings). Other details can then be added to the image to further define the walls, windows or doors. With practice, perspective sketching is a skill that can be quickly acquired.

Constructed perspective drawing is more complex as it requires information from scale plan, section and elevation drawings.

Any perspective representation of a scene that includes parallel lines has one or more vanishing points. A one-point perspective drawing means that the drawing has a single vanishing point, usually directly opposite the viewer's eye and on the horizon. A two-point perspective drawing has parallel lines at two different angles. For example, looking at a house from the corner, one wall would recede towards one vanishing point and the other towards the opposite vanishing point. Three-point perspective is usually used for buildings seen from above or below.

Although constructed perspective drawings appear complex, they do create interesting views of spaces and buildings.

1. & 2. Vanishing point

These before and after images display the critical lines for creating a perspective. The solid line denotes the horizon and the broken lines denote all the lines of view, which converge at the vanishing point.

3. Sketch perspective

This sketch demonstrates the idea of the 'vanishing point'; the image appears to disappear into the centre of the drawing. In reality, the walls of this street never get closer or meet, but to draw the perspective sketch convincingly, the illusion of a vanishing point must be applied.

Three-dimensional images

Three-dimensional images communicate ideas that cannot be conveyed in two-dimensional plan, section and elevation drawings. Drawing in three dimensions gives depth to an image and makes it appear more realistic. Some three-dimensional drawings are sketched and others adopt a more measured approach. Axonometric and isometric three-dimensional drawings, for example, are geometrically constructed.

ISOMETRIC DRAWINGS

Isometric drawings produce three-dimensional images. In these drawings the length, width and height are represented by lines that are 120 degrees apart, with all measurements in the same scale.

To create this type of drawing, a plan, and section and elevation drawings (to scale) of the building or space are required. The plan drawing is then rotated so that it sits at 30 degrees to the horizontal or vertical plane. Placing a piece of tracing paper over the plan will then allow you to redraw the image at the new angle. Lines are then projected vertically from the corners of the redrawn plan; these will represent the height of the building or space. All the measurements are taken from the elevation or section drawings to obtain height, and vertical dimensions should then be transferred to the isometric drawing.

Distorting the plan at 30 degrees to the horizontal or vertical plane makes an isometric drawing more difficult to construct than an axonometric drawing (see page 116), as some initial manipulation is required.

Isometric drawings are useful to describe an internal space or series of larger spaces effectively and explain three-dimensional construction details and assembly drawings.

1., 2. & 3. Isometric drawings
Three-dimensional images enable an understanding of a whole idea and how different spaces can connect to each other. These images show a range of ideas as isometric projections.

116 AXONOMETRIC DRAWINGS

Representation

An axonometric drawing creates a quick three-dimensional projection of a room or space and is produced from a plan drawing. Axonometric drawings are the simplest representational means of achieving a three-dimensional effect.

This type of drawing again requires plan, section and elevation drawings (to scale) of the building or space. The plan drawing is then rotated so that it sits at 45 degrees to the horizontal or vertical plane and is redrawn at this new angle. Using the same approach as with the isometric drawing, lines are then projected vertically from the corners of the redrawn plan and all measurements are taken from the elevation or section drawings and transferred to the axonometric drawing.

Axonometric drawings are quick to produce, but the resultant image, particularly if it is one of a building's exterior, can make the roof appear exaggerated.

Exploded views are a good way of showing detail. These are drawings that appear literally to have been taken apart, and exploded axonometric drawings will explain how a building can be deconstructed and reassembled.

2. Axonometric drawing

This drawing explains an idea as a series of boxes, structure and planar elements.

Physical modelling

Physical models offer another means to show an idea in three-dimensional form. Physical models can take many forms, and can be made from a range of materials and exist at a variety of scales. Just like different drawing types, different model types are used at different stages of the design process to best explain a particular concept or idea.

1. Sectional model
A sectional model at scale 1: 20 reveals the construction idea for a scheme.

2. Site model
A site model contrasts the proposed project with the existing buildings.

3. Urban scale model
This urban scale model illustrates the massing of buildings at various heights on a site.

Different types of physical models are used at different stages of a project's development. In all model types the important issues for consideration are the scale of the model and the materials used to describe the idea. It is not necessary to use the actual intended materials for the project, it is sufficient to just suggest finishes in various ways. However, sometimes using the intended material for the build, such as wood or clay, in the model can strongly communicate the design concept.

Sketch models are quick to construct. They may be produced to scale, or at earlier stages of a project, in a more abstract form, exploring an idea of materials that might be used or a site concept. Sketch models allow the architect to quickly develop a spatial idea.

Concept models use various materials to produce an exaggerated interpretation of an idea or concept. Concept models can be produced at a range of scales and are especially useful at the start of a scheme to explain the direction of the idea. As such, the information they contain needs to be concise and clear.

Detail models explore a specific aspect of an idea, this may be how materials come together at a construction junction or perhaps an interior detail of the finished build. The focus in a detail model is on a single element, not the whole building or architectural concept.

Urban models provide an understanding of a site in the context of its surrounding location. In this type of model the detail is not critical, but the overview is. Urban models provide information about the location of key site elements and the site's topography. The relative position and scale of these elements are important considerations here.

Finished models describe the final architectural idea, and the attention to detail in these models is crucial. Finished models may have roofs or walls that can be removed to describe important aspects of the interior space.

CAD modelling

CAD modelling combines aspects of two- and three-dimensional imaging. CAD software is sufficiently sophisticated to be used at different stages of the design process, from the initial thinking to on-site detailing and implementation. Many software programs require the plan and elevation data in order to produce an accurate set of images. This data is usually a series of coordinates or the length and height measurements of walls with specific parameters.

Computer-aided design (CAD) has made many aspects of building design more efficient. Ideas and drawings can be quickly rendered, revisited, manipulated and revised. Many CAD models allow quick interaction with the viewer and a building can be explored with 'fly-throughs', allowing the viewer to take journeys through the schemes and interact with models of the buildings.

There are many software packages, such as AutoCAD, RealCAD or SolidWorks, which allow the design of elements such as furniture or construction components in two- and three-dimensional forms. Other specialist software allows for the design of buildings and three-dimensional manipulation of the spaces within them. Entire cities can also be designed and visualized using CAD software, allowing an understanding of placing a building on a particular site or location and the impact it may have on adjacent sites.

Rendering packages can provide impressions of realistic material finishes. Other software can help measure and design aspects of shadow, lighting, insulation, structural performance and building energy performance. Each stage of the design process has different specialist programs that can assist with the development and testing of the design idea. Using many of these programs together can provide useful ways to explore a design idea or create a presentation of the complete architectural concept and experience.

1. Pool competition
David Mathias and Peter Williams, 2006
This CAD image was generated for a
swimming-pool scheme and uses computer
graphics to create a dynamic effect.

2. CAD drawing
This drawing is developed using existing site
photos, CAD images for a proposed scheme
and imported images of landscape and
figures to indicate scale.

Physical modelling < **CAD modelling** > Layout and presentation

Layout and presentation

Standard paper sizes determine the size of drawings in a portfolio. In Europe the ISO (International Organization for Standardization) system is used, and this gives a sense of uniformity to hard-copy presentations. In the ISO paper size system, the height-to-width ratio of all pages is the square root of two (1.4142:1). This value underpins the golden section and the Fibonacci sequence.

In terms of appropriate size of layout, there are many factors to consider. Large-scale drawings may need more physical space to be presented, and drawings that need to make an impact may also need to be displayed at a large scale. A smaller-scale drawing will of course be physically smaller and so require less drawing space.

It is critical that the drawing size comfortably accommodates the image at the appropriate scale. Key factors for layout selection are: the actual drawing scale; the intended audience for, or reader of, the drawing;

the clarity of the written information that supports the drawing (such as its title, legend scale, and north point, which is essential on a plan), and the requirement that the size of this supporting information does not distract the reader or viewer from the drawing.

Portrait or landscape layout is another consideration. This choice must relate to other drawings (if the presentation is one of a series of images), and how the format helps the information to be easily read and better understood.

The Fibonacci sequence

0, 1, 1, 2, 3, 5, 8, 13, 21, 34, 55, 89, 144, 23

To create a golden section

A   B   C   D   E

Constructing a golden section

Pictured is the sequence for drawing a golden section. Begin with a square (A) and bisect it (B). Then form a triangle (C) by drawing a line from the bottom of the bisecting line to the top corner of the square. With a compass, extend an arc from the apex of the triangle to the baseline (D) and draw a line perpendicular to the baseline from the point at which the arc intersects it. Complete the rectangle to form the golden section (E).

The golden section (or golden ratio)

The golden section is an irrational number, approximately 1.618, which possesses many interesting properties. Shapes defined by the golden section have long been considered aesthetically pleasing in Western cultures, reflecting nature's balance between symmetry and asymmetry and the ancient Pythagorean belief that reality is a numerical reality. Some studies of the Acropolis, including the Parthenon, conclude that many of its proportions approximate the golden ratio. The Parthenon's façade can be circumscribed by golden rectangles.

Fibonacci numbers

Fibonacci, also known as Leonardo of Pisa, was born in Pisa, Italy (c. 1175). He has been described as a mathematical genius of number theory. He developed the Fibonacci series, in which each consecutive number is the sum of the two preceding numbers (1, 2, 3, 5, 8, 13, 21, 34, 55, 89, 144, etc.). As the series progresses, the ratio of a Fibonacci number divided by the immediately preceding number comes closer and closer to 1.618, the golden section.

77, 610, 987, 1597, 2584, 4181, 6765, 10946

Storyboarding

Storyboarding is a technique often used by film-makers and animators, which can also be used by architects to communicate a plan for a design idea. The storyboard is a very useful tool for designers as it uses captions and incorporates comments and spaces to suggest scenes and activities. The storyboard is a two-dimensional representation of space and time.

1

Destination

Interaction

1. Storyboarding a journey
These annotated images describe a journey through a series of spaces in a city. A storyboard can easily accommodate a series of images and help suggest a narrative or journey that unfolds over time.

Storyboards are used in film-making to create layouts for scenes, bringing together the story, script and location as a plan for the narrative.

Usually, the structure or framework for a storyboard is a series of boxes, which are filled with sketches to describe the characters and events in the narrative. In addition, notes surround these loose sketches, which give further detail about the scene. This level of detail may describe movement or action and contain more information about the surrounding physical environment. The connection between each frame is also important, because it is these connections that bind the story together.

Storyboarding can be a very useful technique for architects because it offers a means to explain how events may take place within their architecture over time. Using the building as a kind of backdrop where potential events might take place is a useful way to plan presentations and pitch architectural concepts and ideas as a kind of narrative or story.

Expression

Determination

Communication

Portfolios

A portfolio is a collection and record of work. For architects, it must satisfy a specific range of requirements and is in itself a design 'project'. Portfolios can take several forms and need to contain a variety of representation techniques to fully explore and represent architectural ideas. They may incorporate concept sketches, orthographic drawings (such as plans, sections and elevations), measured drawings, abstract images, photographs of physical models or CAD images. A portfolio is a kind of narrative that tells a story of your body of work, and before compiling any portfolio for viewing it is essential to know your intended audience.

PHYSICAL PORTFOLIOS

A physical portfolio is traditionally produced in an A1 (594 x 841 mm) format, although A3 (297 x 420 mm) portfolios are sometimes used for more concise presentations. However, the size of portfolio will be determined by the layout chosen and the intended audience.

Portfolios can be produced, revised and adapted for a range of purposes. An academic portfolio is a collection of work produced for a particular course. Professional portfolios may be used to present ideas to a client or to a prospective employer. Other portfolios may be more personal and allow presentation of a body of work or a particular project.

Whatever the intended audience or purpose of the portfolio, the information presented within it needs to be clear and the content edited and carefully planned. Often the portfolio may need to be seen without further supporting material (competition entries, for instance), and in such cases the need for clarity and accurate representation is crucial.

Tips for preparing a portfolio

1. Use a layout technique (such as storyboarding) to plan and organize your portfolio's content.

2. The orientation of the image sheets is very important. Remember a portfolio should read like a book, and sometimes double-page spreads (where two folio sheets read together as one) may be required.

3. Sequencing of drawings is important to accurately tell the story of the building or project from its conception through to final details.

4. The viewer should not have to move to read the work.

To move what?

Representation

1. Student portfolio
This portfolio illustrates the connection of two landscape sheets when opened.

2. Portfolio plan
The layout of a portfolio needs to be designed and the content organized in such a way that it reads as a story, with a beginning, middle and end.

3. Storyboarding
Storyboarding can be used to plan a portfolio layout and provide an overview of the content. This is an outline layout that plans a portfolio as a series of logically progressing pages.

Representation

Electronic portfolios, or e-portfolios, use digital means to produce a CD that can be projected or viewed on a computer. These portfolios are constructed using appropriate software (such as Microsoft's PowerPoint®, for example). To compile an electronic portfolio the images to be displayed must exist in digital form. This may mean that physical models need to be digitally photographed and enhanced and edited in Adobe Photoshop, and drawings that originate in CAD software can again be edited for inclusion in an e-portfolio.

An important consideration here is the means of display for such a collection of images. Are they to be viewed on a computer screen or projected at a much larger scale? The quality, resolution and size of the images will need to be adjusted according to the audience and the way in which the audience will view the material.

A web portfolio is shown via the Internet so it can be viewed or downloaded remotely or by anyone with access to the web.

1. John Pardey Architects
www.johnpardeyarchitects.com
A range of thumbnail images illustrates a wide range of projects, from private houses to larger master-planning schemes. Each image is linked to a range of drawings that explain the project in more detail.

2. Design Engine Architects
www.designengine.co.uk
This web portfolio has a series of clear choices on the home page, identifying four key architectural projects.

3. Panter Hudspith Architects
www.panterhudspith.com
This site uses powerful images on each page, accompanied by clear descriptive text. A local index on the site helps the user to navigate through the range of practice projects.

4. Re-Format
www.re-format.co.uk
Re-Format has an easily navigable website that contains information, images and concepts about each of its projects. The site also includes a blog for news and discussions.

5. Make
www.makearchitects.com
Make uses animated images on their website to create a powerful visual effect. Thumbnail rollover visuals connect the user to additional project information.

Renovation

Project: Department of Philosophy, New York University

Architect: Steven Holl Architects

Client: New York University

Location / date: New York, USA / 2007

There are many ways to describe an architectural project, particularly at the construction phase. Architects use detail drawings to explain how the building is to be assembled by contractors and builders. In addition, sketches can be used to describe spaces, ideas and details.

At the detail design stage, Steven Holl's practice use sketches that are evocative of the intended atmosphere of the space. In addition, these sketches can be annotated by hand to explain a concept or idea. Mixing freehand drawings with other types of line drawings is an excellent way to present architectural ideas. A sketch can supplement measured line drawings, which may be to scale, and can add a different type of dynamic drawing to rigid line drawings.

A sketch can read as a more personal response to a building and can in itself become an original piece of drawn interpretation of a building, like a perspective sketch.

Steven Holl Architects was commissioned by the faculty of Arts and Science at the New York University Department of Philosophy to undertake a complete interior renovation of a historic corner building in Washington Place, New York. The original building dates back to 1890 and is part of the main NYU campus in Greenwich Village. It is located in a historic district of New York and has many preservation orders that restrict its development.

The concept for the scheme was to try to organize the spaces within the building around light coming into the spaces from above, as well as to investigate materials phenomenologically; the idea of the experience of the materials and their sensory qualities. This brief allowed the architect to challenge the existing building and create a dialogue between old and new.

To create a new dynamic in the building, a stair shaft was inserted, allowing light to penetrate down through the six stories of the building. The south-facing stairwell windows have a prismatic film on their surface, which creates a rainbow effect internally as light changes throughout the day.

1. Sketch section through the building
This drawing shows the concept of the light entering through the building and acting conceptually as a vertical connection for the scheme.

NEW LIGHT

Roof Garden

1 6TH FLOOR
6TH FLOOR
MAIN DESK

9'-2" 5TH FLOOR
STEPS:

-8"

4TH FLOOR
STEPS: 22

9"

3RD FLOOR
STEPS: 22

4"

2ND FLOOR
STEPS: 25

4"

1ST FLOOR
STEPS: 28

GRAD STUDENT OFFICE GRAD STUDENT OFFICE GRAD STUDENT OFFICE

GRAD STUDENT OFFICE GRAD STUDENT OFFICE GRAD STUDENT OFFICE

GRAD STUDENT OFFICE GRAD STUDENT OFFICE GRAD STUDENT OFFICE

GRAD STUDENT OFFICE GRAD STUDENT OFFICE GRAD STUDENT OFFICE

GRAD STUDENT OFFICE GRAD STUDENT OFFICE GRAD STUDENT OFFICE

WOOD & COVER RAFT

SOUTH STAIRS
STUDY 02
RISER : 7"
THREAD : 11"

4
26
65
S.H.

CONCEPT: VERTICAL CONNECTIONS IN LIGHT

1. The open foyer space on the ground floor
The existing structure of the historic late nineteenth-century building can still be read alongside the contemporary redesign of the interior.

2. The ground floor space
The students' social spaces on the ground floor have strong visual links to the street.

3. Perforated surfaces
The perforated screen creates a dynamic light quality.

A point of intersection

The ground level, an important facility used by the entire university, serves to connect all areas of the building. As well as the point of entry and exit, it is the intersection and point of movement across and through the building. It offers an important social space for students and has strong visual connections to the street.

On the ground floor, a new wooden auditorium has been inserted that has a curvilinear form, distinctive from the surrounding building in terms of material and form. Various philosophical texts decorate the faculty offices on the upper floors, including Ludwig Wittgenstein's *'Remarks on Colour'*. The idea is that the walls can also inspire some philosophical thinking.

1

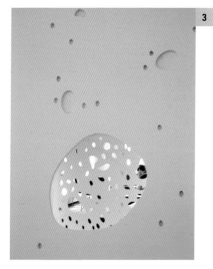

Exercise: Photomontage

Sometimes an architectural idea needs to be placed into an existing view of a site. This is an effective way to suggest how the building may eventually look on its proposed site.

Bringing together a real site image or photo, a sketch idea of a building and then using objects such as trees and street furniture to scale the drawing is an important way to communicate an idea.

For this exercise:

1. Choose a background image and open it in Adobe Photoshop.

2. Make the image black and white.

3. Sketch the proposed building to be edited into the scene and scan this sketch.

4. Import the sketch and delete the white background.

5. Introduce colours and sky into the drawing using the layer transparency settings.

6. Edit images of trees into the foreground of the image and adjust these using the transparency tools.

7. Paste in a selection of people, animals, birds, balloons and so on. If desired, the people can be filled with colour to create silhouettes and the transparency can be adjusted.

8. To complete the image, adjust the brightness and contrast settings and add filters if necessary.

1. Interpretations of the Greater London Authority (GLA) City Hall, London, UK
Foster + Partners
This series of images of the GLA building in London have been adapted to show a variety of impressions of the building.

Representation

Chapter 5
Contemporary Ideas

Within the parameters of this book, contemporary ideas in architecture refer to those of the twentieth and twenty-first century. Architecture is heavily influenced by the zeitgeist (the spirit of the age), but when compared to other aspects of culture, such as art, design or technology, architecture is slower to react. It is not unusual for a large building or public monument to take a decade or longer to be conceived, developed and constructed. Even smaller, domestic-scale buildings, which are often indicative of the lifestyle and fashion of their time, aren't always immediate in their realization.

1. MAXXI National Museum of 21st Century Arts, Rome, Italy
Zaha Hadid Architects, 1998–2009
The spaces inside the MAXXI Museum appear to be sculpted by the concrete forms around them. For more on the MAXXI Museum see the case study on pages 156–159.

1. Plan of the Villa Rotonda, Vicenza, Italy
Andrea Palladio, 1550
Symmetry in architecture symbolizes rational mathematical principles.
Plans for the Villa Rotonda show bilateral symmetry in two directions.
The red lines indicate the axis of symmetry that crosses the villa's
central point.

Universal ideas and principles
There are universal ideas and concepts that transcend style or time and affect all architecture in varying ways. These have been categorized into three groups: geometry, form and route. Within each of these groups, most architecture can be defined or described.

138

GEOMETRY

In this context, geometry describes the ordering and organizing of spaces according to geometric principles. Geometry can affect the plan, elevation or section of a building, as well as its individual elements, such as the doors or windows.

Symmetry is an organizing system that reflects either a plan, or elevation around a central line or axis. An axis connects two or more defined points and can regulate elements such as windows and doors (which will affect experiences such as views and vistas, and the entrance to and exit from buildings).

Proportion describes the relationship of parts to a whole. Within architecture, proportion is the relationship of scale and the hierarchy of a building or structure's elements to its whole form.

3

2. Plan of Château de Versailles, France, Louis Le Vau

This plan of the Château de Versailles displays the relationship of the château (designed by architect Louis Le Vau) to the gardens (designed by landscape architect André Le Notre) and demonstrates strong systems of symmetry along an axis. Within each of the parterre gardens, other symmetrical patterns exist. The red lines here indicate the main organizing axis of both garden and house.

3. Plan of Villa Stein, Garches, France Le Corbusier

The seemingly irregular plan of Le Corbusier's Villa Stein is governed by the precise geometric proportioning system of a modular grid. The numbers shown relate to the module measurement that is applied to both the plan and the elevation of the building, which creates a certain rhythm.

Universal ideas and principles > Functionalism

1. Plan of the Temple of Horus
This Egyptian temple, whose design is attributed to Ptolemy III and dates from 237–57 BC, consists of an inner sanctuary that is surrounded by a series of wrapping walls and colonnaded entrance courtyards and halls. The plan of the building reads as a series of layers around the central protected space.

2. Plan of Richards Medical Centre, Philadelphia, USA
Louis Kahn
One of Louis Kahn's principal ideas was the distinction between 'served' and 'servant' spaces. The Richards Medical Centre in Philadelphia, USA, exemplifies this ideal. The glass-walled workrooms are 'served' by separate, free-standing brick chimneys. Each 'served' space has an independent structural frame with a complete set of supports and its own source of natural illumination.

140 FORM

Contemporary Ideas

Architectural concepts can be expressed using simple terms that characterize the form or shape of a building. Some forms are dynamic, sculptural and strongly influenced by the external appearance of the building. This category of design idea is described as 'function following form'. Other building forms are more practical, determined by the internal activities or purpose of the building. These ideas can be described as those of 'form following function'.

'Servant served' is a description that Louis Kahn used to describe the different categories of space in a building, whether a small-scale house or a large-scale civic building. Servant spaces have functional use, such as storage rooms, bathrooms or kitchens – the spaces that are essential for a building to function properly. Served spaces might be living or dining rooms or offices – spaces that the servant areas serve. This concept provides a very useful way to understand the organization of a building.

Louis Kahn 1901–1974
Originally from Estonia, Kahn grew up in New York but he remained influenced by European classical architecture. Kahn was very interested in materials and their relationship to form, and was fascinated by the notions of served and servant spaces and the hierarchies in building plans.

His most important buildings are the Yale Art Gallery in Connecticut, USA, the Richards Medical Centre in Philadelphia, USA, the Kimbell Art Museum in Texas, USA, and the National Assembly Building in Dhaka, Bangladesh.

**3. Drawing of Villa Savoye, Paris, France
Le Corbusier**

Le Corbusier celebrated the journey around and the route through the Villa Savoye, using ramps and stairs to connect the movement around the building with the views and vistas from it. Enfilade (taken from the French, meaning to thread or to pass through from end to end) refers to a suite of rooms with doorways that align with one another. The Villa Savoye is planned in this way so that the rooms also connect and open up to create a journey through the building.

**4. Plan of the Château de Versailles, France
Louis Le Vau**

This plan of the Château de Versailles provides an example of enfilade planning; it incorporates a series of rooms that are connected together along an axis.

ROUTE

The route through a building is an important organizational tool. The route from outside a building's door or entrance into the building will be any visitor's first experience of the architecture. How this journey then continues through the building, the connections between the outside and the inside and through and between the different interior levels, will further enhance the experience.

In some buildings, such as museums and galleries, this route may be designed as part of the architectural concept. The route through these buildings might allow, in this instance, the art or artefacts to be better understood and experienced. Buildings can also have strong relationships to the journeys or routes around them; a promenade, for example, celebrates the movement around a building or structure both inside and outside the building.

Functionalism

'Form follows function' was a phrase coined by American architect **Louis Sullivan**. It described a means of redirecting architecture and followed the premise that the form of any building should be defined by the activities that were to be carried out inside it, rather than any historical precedent or aesthetic ideal. Sullivan designed the world's first skyscrapers using these functionalist design principles. The concept of functionalism was further developed by Austrian architect Adolf Loos. He wrote of 'ornament as crime', and was a proponent of the argument that any superfluous decoration on a building was unnecessary. The thinking of both architects contributed towards new and modern responses to architectural design.

MODERNISM

Modernism was a huge architectural influence in the twentieth century and, as its name suggests, the modernist movement embraced the contemporary modern culture. Modernism interacted with a dynamic that brought together political, social and cultural changes. Expressive minimal and organic styles can refer to modernism in some way.

Modernist architecture is a term given to a number of building styles with similar characteristics, primarily the simplification of form and the elimination of ornament, which first arose around 1900. The modernist architects responded to the concepts of 'form following function' and 'ornament as crime', adopting forms that derived from the response to the functions or activities within the buildings, and leaving the buildings devoid of any adornment or unnecessary decoration, producing characteristically clean white spaces.

By the 1940s, these styles had been consolidated and became the dominant architectural style for institutional and corporate building for several decades in the twentieth century.

1. Isokon Lawn Road flats, London, UK
Wells Coates, 1934
These apartments were purposefully
designed using the application of
modernist principles. The architecture
is bright, practical and very functional,
and the furniture was also purpose-
designed for the interior spaces. These
apartments also incorporated some of
the UK's first examples of fitted
kitchens, which offered potential
occupants a practical and
contemporary lifestyle.

2. Villa Savoye (interior), Paris, France
Le Corbusier, 1928–1929
Le Corbusier's Villa Savoye introduced
a new type of open-plan building. Its
light interior spaces and the absence
of any decoration or adornment
presented a practical, simple and
functional approach to living.

Louis Sullivan 1856–1924
An American architect, Sullivan is most notably associated with the design of the skyscraper, which became a real possibility when the
development of steel-framed buildings and construction technology advanced (the Carson Pirie Scott and Company department store in
Chicago is Sullivan's most famous steel-framed building). His approach was concerned with 'form following function' and the buildings he
produced were driven by functional necessity.

1. The Farnsworth House, Illinois, USA
Ludwig Mies van der Rohe, 1946–1951
The Farnsworth House is one of the more famous examples
of modernist domestic architecture and was considered
unprecedented in its day. Transcending any traditional domestic
function, the importance of this house lies in the absolute purity
and consistency of its architectural idea.

1

144 THE MODERNIST FOUNDERS

Contemporary Ideas

By the 1920s, the most important figures in modern
architecture had established their reputations. The three
'founders' are commonly recognized as Le Corbusier in
France, and Ludwig Mies van der Rohe and Walter
Gropius in Germany.

Mies van der Rohe and Gropius were both directors
of the Bauhaus School (1919–1938), one of a number
of European schools and associations concerned with
reconciling craft tradition and industrial technology.
The Bauhaus was one of the most influential schools of
architecture, art and design of the twentieth century. Its
pedagogy required a new approach, one that explored the
functionality and practicality of design, housed workshops
and studios, and taught architecture through aspects of
contemporary culture, film, dance, art and product design.
The Bauhaus promoted a new unity between art and
technology, and encouraged thinking and designs that
responded to both technology and ideology.

Form-driven architecture

The modernist approach, which saw the function of a building affect its final shape and form, was to produce a reactive and opposing school of architectural thought. Sculpturalism dictates that function follows form; that the shape of a building should be the architect's primary consideration, and that any functions and activities the building is to house should be accommodated into this form.

Many such buildings have become so iconic that they have become associated with the brand of a city or place. These buildings tend to have a very strong sculptural or iconic form; the architecture is distinctive.

Organic architecture describes a design approach where the form is dominant and is influenced by fluid and dynamic shapes. The construction of this type of structural form can usually only be achieved using innovative materials and cutting-edge technology to assist with the design of the spaces and the manufacture of the building. One of the earliest architects who embraced the ideals of organic architecture was Antoni Gaudí; his most famous works La Sagrada Familia and the Parc Güel (both in Barcelona, Spain) use forms in a sculptural way to great dynamic effect.

Sculptural architecture is also exemplified by the work of Frank Gehry and his use of materials in groundbreaking and jaw-dropping ways. Gehry's architectural ideas are initially created and designed using a sculptural process too. Sculptural architecture works well with flexible materials and a fine example of this is Gehry's Guggenheim Museum in Bilbao, Spain. The museum uses heavy limestone blocks at the base, and titanium metal sheets, which curve and reflect light, form the walls and the roof. The combination of materials and the forms that they

are made to adopt creates a striking contrast with the rectilinear forms of the city.

Both sculptural and organic design approaches require all the activities of a building to be fitted into the dramatic shape or form. In the best examples of this architecture, the interior and exterior experience work together to impressive effect.

1. La Sagrada Familia, Barcelona, Spain
Antoni Gaudi, still to be completed
La Sagrada Familia is extremely ornamental and decorative. It looks like it has been sculpted rather than built. Its stones appear almost liquid-like and display a light, open quality. This challenges our preconceptions of a heavy stone structure.

2. Frederick R. Weisman Art Museum, Minneapolis, USA
Frank Gehry, 1993
This museum is a great example of function following form. Gehry's architecture uses the form primarily to determine the building; its materiality and shape are the main considerations.

3. & 4. Student work
Student experiments with material to create sculpted forms.

Contemporary Ideas

2

SCULPTURAL INTERIORS

Buildings can have dramatic exteriors as well as organic or sculptural forms, and can also contain an interior experience that is equally dynamic. Floors, walls and ceilings can challenge convention and slope inward or outward to great theatrical effect. Sloped ceilings and floor planes working together can create an incredibly exaggerated effect, extending the sense of perspective inside a space. Equally, walls can be constructed to exaggerate the perceived height of a space. This creates an architectural illusion; our perception of these spaces is altered through careful use of material and form.

This type of building creates unexpected encounters, sloping floors and leaning walls, for example, produce a gravity-defying experience. In such a building, everything needs to be reconsidered, from the lighting and furniture, to the apertures for walls and windows. The relationship from the outside to the inside of the architecture is particularly dramatic. New types of lightweight composite materials have made architecture of this sort a real possibility.

1. Phaeno Science Center, Wolfsburg, Germany
Zaha Hadid, 2000–2005
This building challenges conventional and traditional shapes and forms and is typical of Zaha Hadid's ideas, which are both sculptural and dynamic. The Phaeno Science Center is a new paradigm for architecture; dynamic shapes are formed as the building acts like a landscape, with the different levels of the exhibition space positioned at different heights within it. The spaces challenge most preconceived ideas about a building; it is almost impossible to determine where the walls stop and where the floor or ceiling begins.

2. Visualization of a sports centre project, student work
This scheme by a third year architecture student shows an interior view of a sports centre project. The concept for the roof is a sculpted surface that reflects natural light.

Monumentalism

A building that is monumental has meaning beyond its form and function. It can be monumental both in its scale and in what it represents. Monuments have been constructed to celebrate important events and people for centuries. Some of these structures are still part of our culture today; think of Stonehenge in the UK or the pyramids at Giza. Buildings that become synonymous with more than their function, perhaps with a city or a culture, could be described as monumental. Monumental buildings may not be occupied; rather, they can be symbolic in terms of what they represent.

HYBRID

Some buildings have become synonymous with their location and the identity of it. If one considers any major city, it's possible to think of a building or structure associated with it, the White House in Washington, Buckingham Palace in London or the Musée du Louvre in Paris, for example. All these buildings have meaning associated with them beyond their architecture. They have become icons of their location.

There is another, more contemporary, idea of a building or space that works as a monument and also celebrates an important event or is a place for cultural events to take place (and/or has a cultural or national significance). Examples of these include Times Square, the Sydney Opera House, the Eiffel Tower and Trafalgar Square. Such buildings or spaces can be described as having a dual purpose or are hybrid in terms of their definition.

Parliament buildings also fall into the category of monumental architecture as they have a national symbolism and often connect with a cultural identity. A new parliament building needs to represent a nation in terms of its architectural form, its materiality and its presence.

The German parliament building, the Reichstag, uses materials that reinforce architectural and political metaphors. This nineteenth-century building was redesigned and reinterpreted by Foster + Partners in 1999 and its architecture is underpinned by a transparent structure, which is intended to reflect the ideal of a transparent, open and modern democracy in government. The glass-domed structure has a ramp within it, so one can look down from above into the debating chamber, to watch the activity of parliament. The Reichstag building was a symbol of reunification and the reinvention of modern Germany.

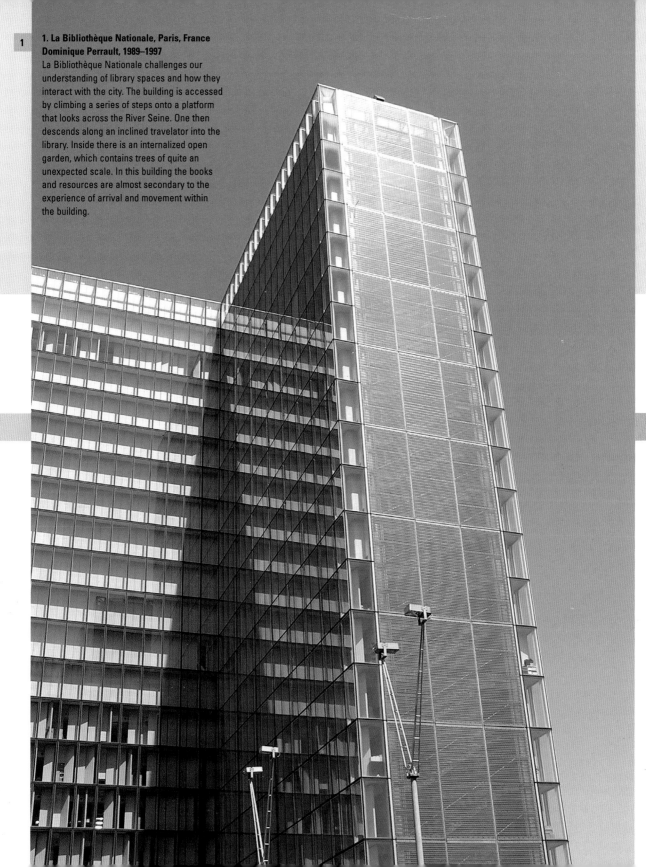

1. La Bibliothèque Nationale, Paris, France
Dominique Perrault, 1989–1997
La Bibliothèque Nationale challenges our understanding of library spaces and how they interact with the city. The building is accessed by climbing a series of steps onto a platform that looks across the River Seine. One then descends along an inclined travelator into the library. Inside there is an internalized open garden, which contains trees of quite an unexpected scale. In this building the books and resources are almost secondary to the experience of arrival and movement within the building.

Zeitgeist

The German term 'zeitgeist' refers to the spirit of a time. In terms of design, this is an inevitably changing and shifting notion. The zeitgeist naturally evolves as it responds to current social and cultural phenomena. A building can encapsulate a moment in history and have a longevity that allows it to survive through many cultural generations.

At the beginning of the twentieth century, design was responding to modernist ideals and approaches. The modernist style and its use of materials and form originated in Europe and, although not applicable in all contexts, had enormous influence in other regions across the world. The concept of an 'international' style was based on the notion that a style or design could exist across many cultures and have no boundaries.

One of the perceived strengths of the international style was that the design solutions were indifferent to location, site, and climate. This was one of the reasons it was called 'international'; the style made no reference to local history or national vernacular. Later, this was identified as one of the style's primary weaknesses.

The modernist style has, however, been adapted by some to accommodate local conditions. Examples of this are Oscar Niemeyer's architecture in Brazil and Luis Barragan's work in Mexico. Their style is modern in form, but uses bolder form and colour as it is influenced by local traditions.

1. Munich Airport Centre (MAC), Munich, Germany
Murphy Jahn Architects, 1989–1999
The Munich Airport Centre defines the airport in an era of globalization. It is a place in itself, a destination that integrates transportation, commerce, technology and landscape. There is a relationship between travel, work, shopping and entertainment that allows the airport to become a complete architectural experience.

2. The National Congress, Brasilia, Brazil
Oscar Niemeyer, 1958–1960
Niemeyer organized a competition for the urbanistic layout of Brasilia and the winner was a proposal from his old master and friend, Lúcio Costa. Niemeyer would design the buildings and Lúcio the plan of the city.

Taking his lead from modernist ideals, Niemeyer designed a large number of residential, commercial and government buildings. Among them were the residence of the President, the House of the Deputy, the National Congress, as well as many residential buildings. Viewed from above, the city can be seen to have elements that repeat themselves in every building, giving it a formal unity.

Meier has a consistent approach and style
to his architecture. The cool, white light
qualities and distinct areas of shadow in
the spaces create interest. He has designed
many galleries that are distinctive and
provide a white neutral background against
which to read the artworks.

154 MATERIALS

To understand the possibilities and limitations of materials
is an important aspect of architecture. Whether it be an
understanding of both contemporary and historical uses
of a material, or the testing of an innovative approach to
its application or use, this knowledge informs and
underpins the design process.

The material quality of a building has to relate to its site
and environment (the exterior), and to its function and
users (the interior). These are very different requirements,
but the specification of the materials must reconcile the
interior and exterior demands of the building. To learn
how to develop this skill, it is important for architects to
see how materials need to sit together, are fixed together
and how they can coexist and complement one another.

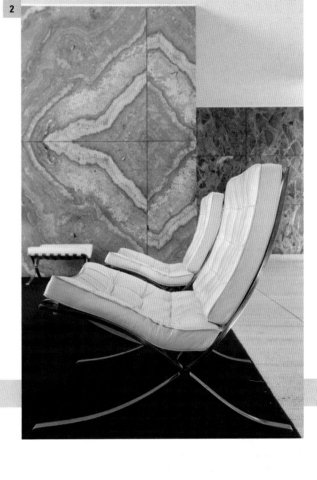

2. The Barcelona Pavilion (interior)
Ludwig Mies van der Rohe, 1928–1929
This is an interior detail of a marble wall
inside the Barcelona Pavilion. The pavilion
was built from glass, travertine and
different kinds of marble.

STYLE

Style represents a response to culture and can be viewed
as a kind of fashion or popular trend. In architecture, as in
many other cultural art forms, very often these styles are
referred to as 'isms'. Classicism is a style informed by
classical architecture and culture. Similarly, modernism
was influenced by modern culture of the 1920s and 1930s.

Labels that attach themselves to these styles are varied.
Some are very particular while others are much looser.
It is important to appreciate the affect that each 'ism' has
had on succeeding styles and to remember that all design
comes from an understanding of precedent, whether
historic, cultural or social. The invention and originality
of design comes from its application and timing in
contemporary culture: its appropriateness for now.

The question of style is a difficult issue for architecture
generally, as it has aesthetic as well as functional
parameters. If architecture is too attached to
contemporary style, it will quickly appear 'unfashionable',
which is problematic as architecture needs to be durable.
The most enduring architectural concepts and ideas have
accommodated changing cultures, users and functions.

Integrating with an urban landscape

Project: Museo delle arti del XXI secolo (MAXXI) / National Museum of the 21st Century Arts

Architect: Zaha Hadid Architects

Culture: Italian Ministry of Culture

Location / date: Rome, Italy / 1998–2009

Contemporary ideas represent the latest thinking in architectural expression and capture the zeitgeist, or 'spirit of the time' in terms of architectural thinking. Architecture needs to respond to ideas that may originate in many areas of society, or be influenced by art, sculpture or technologies.

Zaha Hadid's architecture is very distinctive; it is sculptural in form, both on the outside and also in terms of the interior experience. Hadid's practice uses materials in new ways that work with this sculptural expression. The spaces she designs need to be experienced three-dimensionally; they challenge conventional ideas of space and form.

For example, Hadid's Museo delle arti del XXI secolo (MAXXI), or the National Museum of 21st Century Arts, in Rome, is about texture and light, and the idea of an iconic building that is stylistically and experientially distinctive.

The MAXXI Museum in Rome was completed in 2010. The concept of the project was to respond to the surrounding urban landscape, to make a connection to the ground level at certain points and at others to become distinct and separate.

The main route into the building is from a road that connects the local area to the nearby River Tiber. Taking this link with a major waterway as a starting point, the building's design is full of connections beyond the limitations of the contained site. Circulation routes within the building carry on as routes outside the museum, tying the building into the surrounding city.

The architectural elements that project formally from the building are also connected to geometric orders outside the building, connecting to urban grids that inform the roadways and pathways in Rome. This relationship to the city is a key defining characteristic of the building; relating internal and external circulation. The building is designed to be more than a signature cultural object, instead it belongs to the city that surrounds it. The building is part of the topographical landscape of the city: part of the public space.

The spaces within the museum are defined by strong formal architectural elements to create a strong canvas or backdrop against which to juxtapose the artwork that is displayed within. The building offers a dynamic background for the objects of the gallery.

The gallery comprises a long exhibition space that snakes through the building, creating a kind of labyrinth experience or journey. The space uses a dynamic set of curves and is itself a sculptural element within the building. The artwork is not mounted on the wall, but is instead attached to adjustable partitions to ensure the exhibitions have a separate identity from the building.

The building uses concrete confidently and effectively to create a dynamic background to the artwork.

Movement through and across the building, and its relationship to movement through and across the surrounding city context was the conceptual driver for the project.

1

1. Building section of the National Museum of 21st Century Arts, Rome, Italy
Zaha Hadid Architects
The section through the building illustrates the double height spaces and the relationship of the gallery area to the rest of the building.

1. & 2. Internal light
The interior spaces are carefully lit; the natural light highlights the texture of the concrete surface.

3. & 4. Material contrast
The white panels of the exhibition walls contrast with the concrete walls and structure.

5. Contrasting external forms
The external form of the building is sculptural and dynamic, reading as a massive element balanced on a structural wall beneath.

6. & 7. Light and movement
The concrete structure inside determines the flow and movement through the building, the stairs are emphasized by artificial lighting.

Chapter 5

Exercise: Analytical diagrams

Designing buildings is about understanding concepts; the starting point of the architecture. Concepts are best explained as simple diagrams and drawings. However, translating a concept into a simple drawing is quite a challenge.

To start to understand how buildings are designed, basic ideas that generate buildings, such as geometry, access and route, can be analysed on a set of drawings to help you to simplify ideas.

For this exercise:

Take a plan or section and trace over it. Identify key theories within the design – such as promenade, routes, access, exits from buildings, servant and served spaces, wrapping walls, free planes, thick walls and layers – and consider the hierarchy of these elements. Try to draw the buildings as simply as possible.

The example on page 161 shows drawings of the Barcelona Pavilion by Mies van der Rohe. The key ideas identified within this building are the wrapping walls and free planes, which are expressed as walls and a roof that appear to float.

The building is designed as a simple structural frame that allows the walls to be considered as non-structural simple planes. This allows a flexibility for the position of walls, roofs, openings and surfaces within the building.

1. Analytical diagrams of the Barcelona Pavilion
The Barcelona Pavilion is analysed here as a set of diagrams
to describe the architectural ideas that are comprised within the
building.

1

This chapter explores an architectural project, 6a Architects' refurbishment of the South London Gallery, from inception through to completion, showing the stages through which an architectural project is realized. This project helps to demonstrate the important synthesis of ideas and considerations that come together in the architecture of a building.

This process of synthesis is a type of journey; there is a narrative attached to the making of a building, from its initial concept to the finished construction. Following a project through each of these stages will show that a diverse range of skills is involved, from conceptual thinking to practical construction.

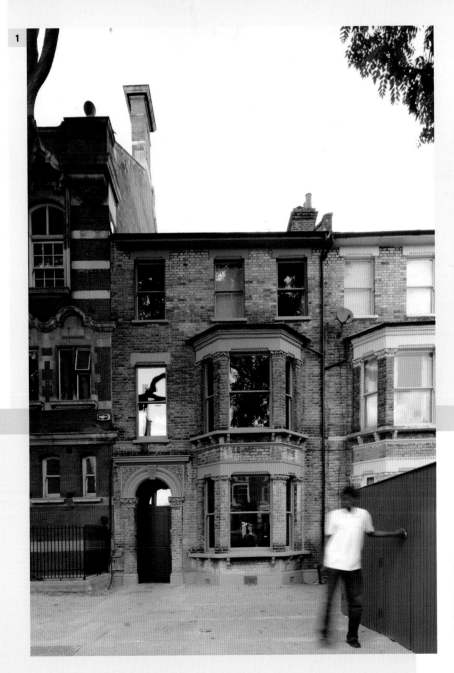

**1. South London Gallery (SLG), UK
6a Architects 2010**
The exterior of the derelict house
adjacent to the South London Gallery
(SLG), which 6a Architects refurbished
and incorporated into the life of
the museum.

1. Concept (page 172)

i. Section through the building.
a: No. 67, derelict terrace house.
b: New triple-height extension.
c: The New Clore Education Studio.

2. Site analysis (page 174)

ii. The site before construction.

iii. The existing brick wall revealed.

iv. The timber frame exposed during construction.

3. The design process (page 176)

4. Detail development (page 178)

5. The finished building (page 180)

Realization

Project timeline

Projects vary depending on time and complexity, but in each case their realization represents a journey that tells the story of how a building is made. This timeline shows a set of five key stages of a project's realization: concept, site analysis, the design process, construction and detail development and the result. Each of the sections identified in the timeline will be described in more detail later in the chapter.

vii

v. The ground floor plan. (a: derelict house, b: triple-height extension, c: The Clore Education Studio).

vi. The first floor plan.

vii. The roof plan.

xi

viii. The Clore Education Studio at the rear of the site.

ix. The wall opening to the garden.

x. The new space under construction.

xi. The stair of no. 67 with dynamic artwork suggesting movement.

xv

xii. New fittings at no. 67, updated but still reflecting the original domestic scale of the building.

xiii. This was part of a range of artwork incorporated as a temporary installation to mark the inaugural exhibition.

xiv. Temporary artwork by Ernst Caramelle, commissioned by SLG as part of the inaugural exhibition.

xv. The study room with gold leaf design by Paul Morrison.

The project

This project involves the expansion of the South London Gallery (SLG), a small gallery in South East London, founded in 1891. The gallery presents contemporary art exhibitions and live art events, with integrated education projects. The expansion of the gallery was designed by 6a Architects, an international practice based in London. Their brief was to expand the SLG to incorporate new gallery spaces, a café, a flat for an artist-in-residence and a new education building. They achieved this through three interventions. Firstly, they refurbished a neighbouring derelict house to incorporate the café, artist-in-residence accommodation and new exhibition space. They also added a three-storey extension to the back of the house that links with the main gallery building, the whole extension was renamed the 'Matsudaira Wing'.

They also designed a new education building, called The Clore Education Studio, which utilized the brick walls of an old lecture theatre that had been destroyed in the Second World War. The design incorporated two surviving walls from the lecture theatre and acts as a link to the new Fox Garden behind the site, joining it with the gallery's existing garden.

1

1. Examples of the existing spaces and materials.

2. The original street façade of the building.

3. The original plans of the building. The section marked 'a' denotes the original gallery space. The section marked 'b' shows the site of the new Clore Education Studio, which incorporates two walls from a lecture theatre partially destroyed in the Second World War.

Contributors and their roles

The realization of any project will involve a vast team of people, and each member of that team will have different skills that can be applied at different stages of the design and construction processes. Central to the success of any architectural project will be ensuring that the team works well together and that the necessary project information is communicated clearly among all members of the team.

The roles described below are a general list of the project team. Some projects are small and require fewer team players. More specialized projects will need a range of contributors, from project managers to specialist engineers, at various stages of the project.

THE CLIENT

The client initiates the project, provides the funds for construction and is usually the building's end user. The best clients will have aspirations for their building, and these will be translated clearly into a range of activities and functionality that they want the architecture to accommodate. For example, they may have a vision in terms of what internal and external environments they expect the building to provide them with, or have expectations about what the building needs to symbolize or represent.

All these requirements, desires and functions will then be shaped into a project brief, which is used by the architect as a springboard and measure of their design ideas.

SURVEYORS

Surveyors measure different aspects of a building. A building surveyor measures the material and fabric of the architecture and produces drawings of an existing building on site or of the location and levels of extant site features. The information in these drawings allows the site parameters to be better understood before the architect begins to consider the building's design. For example, if the site is sloped, this will affect what it is possible to build.

Building surveyors can also be involved in establishing boundaries of sites and buildings. Specialists such as historic building surveyors have specific knowledge of older buildings, which can also be valuable.

A quantity surveyor measures the building's materials and, by itemizing and costing all these, provides an estimate of the project costs. Together with the brief and survey drawings, these projections are used to form the contract or instructions that will indicate how the building is to be constructed.

ENGINEERS

Engineers are concerned with the technical application of scientific understanding to design. They design systems in conjunction with the architect, whether it is the building's structure or its heating, ventilation or electrical solutions.

Structural engineers work with the various aspects of a building's structure, including the frame, the foundations and the façades. They advise, inform and design structural aspects of the building, from its overall frame through to individual details such as the size of structural supports or fixings. A structural engineer will demonstrate the viability of the building and rationalize its structural elements so that they are efficient, effective and so that they complement the overall architectural idea.

A mechanical engineer is, broadly, someone who is involved with the design, development and installation of machinery. In building terms, this refers to the designer of the building's mechanical, heating and ventilation systems. These systems need to be considered, specific and integrated into the design idea so that they work effectively with the spatial material and formal architectural concepts.

Electrical engineers work very closely with the mechanical engineers to design and oversee the installation of the electrical systems for the building. On larger projects, electrical engineers can work with lighting consultants to provide a specific lighting strategy for the building.

Acoustic engineers deal with aspects of noise control. They understand how sounds move through the building's materials, and can suggest specifications that will affect the user's experience of sound in the building. When buildings need to accommodate many and varied functions, acoustic engineers can advise about separation of structures, such as walls or floors, to reduce sound transmission. Additionally they can advise on material specifications that can alter sound appreciation in space.

LANDSCAPE ARCHITECTS

All architecture is positioned in a location or context; landscape architects are concerned with connecting a building to its surroundings.

Landscape architects will start by analysing the site to understand specific climatic conditions, such as rainfall, amount of sunlight or temperature range, and to understand the area's indigenous plants and their planting conditions.

Landscape design also considers aspects of the journey and route through the building's external spaces, and the activities associated with those spaces. Good landscape design binds a building into its site, complements all aspects of the architecture and is inseparable from the building.

CONTRACTORS

Building contractors physically construct the building, working with information provided by engineers, architects and surveyors. Generally, they are directed by a project manager or architect on site. Some projects may also obtain the services of subcontractors or specialists to make something in a particular way or using a special technique.

Building contractors adhere to a schedule of works that they devise at the start of the project to ensure that the materials, tradesmen and services are all coordinated to allow the building project to progress smoothly. The integration of these different services is critical to the successful completion of the building.

The brief

The brief is written to limit and define the project specifications, determining aspects of function, construction, materiality and relationship to site. The brief is composed initially as a response to the client's intentions for the site, and is then further developed to provide detailed information about the project requirements, including, among other factors, appraisal of site, accommodation requirements, internal layout requirements and specialized fittings and fixtures.

When 6a Architects were commissioned to refurbish a derelict Victorian house neighbouring the South London Gallery (SLG), the brief from the client was to enhance the visitor experience by providing additional gallery spaces, a flat for a programme of artist residencies and a café. In addition, 6a were asked to design an education studio at the rear of the site. The new education space was required to enable the gallery to work with thousands of people every year on site.

The brief also specified that the expansion of the gallery into the Victorian house should be achieved without losing the 'soul' of the original building, and without it being overwritten as an institutional building. The conversion design therefore needed to retain the house's character, bring it into the life of the gallery and provide new stimulating spaces for visitors.

6a achieved this remarkably successfully, and the site has been opened up and released by the project. The architects' intention was to retain a 'domestic' scale space, which is in keeping with the existing character of the building. As 6a explains, they achieved this by allowing the new spaces to 'follow the arrangement of the original front and back rooms, but the architectural language is abstracted and reduced like an image faded through time.'

The brief also called for the new Fox Garden room to become a key space and its design and execution were central to the success of the conversion. It is residential in scale, but grand, tall and public in character, taking the visitor from the house into the larger public spaces.

1. The study room
The study room, with a double-height ceiling, looks out over the new 'Fox Garden' and includes gold leaf artwork by Paul Morrison. The SLG commissioned the gold leaf piece as part of the inaugural temporary installation, but decided to keep it as a permanent addition to the room.

The concept

The concept is the driving idea of the project and it will respond to the architecture's function, site and brief, as well as any historic or typological precedents.

Developing the concept from sketch to a fully functional building, one that refers back to and connects with the initial ideas, is a challenge. Because of this, concepts for architectural projects need to be clearly understood by all members of the team so that they can inform and be reinforced at all stages of the project's development.

THE PROJECT CONCEPT

The project concept was an integrated, sensitive response to a historic building. The greatest challenge for 6a was to extend the South London Gallery without alienating those who cherished the existing building; they did this by leaving the main space precisely intact by creating a series of three interventions dispersed around an expanded site. A new sequence of fully accessible interior and exterior spaces significantly enlarged the range of possible activities and events, while establishing an unexpected and inspiring architectural dialogue between old and new, inside and outside.

In restoring and extending the neighbouring house to form the new Matsudaira Wing, great care was taken to retain the intimacy of the domestic environment and to retain the original features within the contemporary re-building.

1. Refurbishing a domestic space

One of the major challenges with refurbishing the derelict house adjacent to the South London Gallery, was incorporating the domestic space into a public arena, without losing its original intimate character. 6a struck this balance perfectly with key elements such as the carefully detailed staircase with artwork by Gary Woodley.

2. Section drawing

The proposed section drawing across the new building cutting through the courtyard space showing the relationship from inside to outside.

a: No. 67, the original derelict house refurbished to include a cafe and gallery spaces.

b: The new Garden Room.

c: The Fox Garden.

d: The New Clore Education Studio.

Site analysis

Site analysis is a process that allows for specific aspects of the project's location to inform the design idea. For example, there may be historical precedents, in terms of building design or construction techniques, which are particular to that locality; or climate ranges and average temperatures that may affect the relationship between a building's interior and exterior. All these factors, and more, can affect the design ideas.

Analysing and understanding the immediate locality and the surrounding area will allow the design to better connect with both the site and its context.

The South London Gallery (SLG) was built in 1891 behind the cottage of its founder, William Rossiter, which stood along rural Peckham Road. In 1905, the cottage was demolished to make way for Camberwell College of Arts, which stands there today. The SLG, widely regarded as one of the finest exhibition spaces in London, is an elegant rectangular volume with a large roof light over the centre.

The main space is impressive in scale, but invisible from the street and the long, narrow corridor leading to it adds to the sense of surprise upon entering. The special character of the building has long inspired artists and as such it has played a vital role in forming the SLG's international reputation for shows by contemporary British artists such as Ryan Gander, Steve McQueen, Eva Rothschild and Michael Landy, alongside those by internationally established figures such as Chris Burden and Alfredo Jaar.

The proportions and construction of the derelict house and garden adjacent to the SLG were starkly different from the elegance of the gallery. 6a's challenge was to marry a public building with a domestic home to produce a unified space that fulfilled a variety of roles.

1. The garden before construction work.

2. The materials of the original building revealed.

"The concept < **Site analysis** > The design process"

1

2

The design process

The process of designing a building is an unpredictable journey. It starts as a concept, perhaps represented as a series of sketches or some models, but as the idea develops, key considerations and decisions have to be made by the client. These will concern the use of individual spaces, the functional requirements of the building and its surroundings, the use of materials, or the heating, ventilation and lighting strategies. The decisions taken on such issues should reinforce the initial architectural concept. During the design process it is vital that the key concept is retained and that any decision-making does not compromise the integrity of the idea.

Realization

For 6a Architect's work on the South London Gallery (SLG), the project design process involved working closely with the client to appreciate their ambitions to ensure that the art remained accessible and part of an integrated experience for the public. It was also key to ensure that original aspects of the building, including its structure and material, remained an important characteristic of the interior.

The original raw timber roof structure has been exposed and painted white, making reference to the house's formerly derelict state but also echoing the far grander exposed trusses of the main gallery space. This inspired the motif for the new buildings – a double-height room linking the house to the main space, and the Clore Studio at the rear of the main building – which gradually transforms from the domesticity of the house to the civic grandeur of the main gallery.

Other motifs carried throughout the new buildings suggest unity through the diverse spaces, equally lending them distinctive character. Areas of brickwork have been painted or left bare; tiles have been laid in a diagonal pattern both inside and out and an emphasis on light is evident throughout.

Surprising views on to, between and through the different spaces, both inside and out, reveal the maze-like quality of the cluster of linked buildings, adding interest and drawing visitors from one area through to the next. On the upper floors, vistas through windows and from the roof terrace of the artist's flat also highlight the SLG's very particular location in the heart of an inner city area, wedged between a turn-of-the-century art college and a 1950s housing estate.

1, 2. & 3. Plans of the ground, first and second floors of the building.

1

2

3

Detail development

At this stage in the project, drawings are produced to allow the building to be constructed. These drawings will vary in scale and number; bespoke elements will need lots of detail to explain construction whereas other, more standard, aspects of construction will need little detailed explanation or drawings.

1

PROJECT DETAIL DEVELOPMENT

The South London Gallery (SLG) project required sensitivity to the existing materials. There needed to be careful attention to detail, linking the old and new features of the building. The new elements of the building complement and contrast with the existing building, and the new materials have a softness that work well alongside the heavy Victorian brick building.

The new Clore Education Studio is made from a lightweight timber and steel frame clad in light tiles, which blend easily with the London brick, but contrast as light contemporary materials. There is a steel frame roof light that floods the space with light from above. In addition it has carefully designed pivoting doors that transform the garden wall into an open edge in the summer, softening the threshold between inside and outside. The result is a space that flows easily between the gallery and the garden.

The interior is treated simply to act as a discrete backdrop to the gallery, painted white walls reflecting light internally. All surfaces have been carefully considered to ensure the internal spaces, although small in scale, appear light and open.

FORTRESS EUROPE

I PUT A
SPILL ON
YOU

G-8
G-20
G-SPOT

CRY CRY
CRISIS

ASH

BUDGET
CUT

BEER

OIL

ON
OFF

PROFIT

FIRE
BERLIN WALL

EXIT STRA

1. Part of the finished refurbished building, with original details still clearly evident.

2. The new Clore Education Studio featuring artwork by Dan Perjovschi (commissioned by the SLG).

The finished building

All architecture needs to be imagined by the architect at the start of the project. The interesting aspect of any project is how well this imagined idea connects with the realized building. There are always aspects of architecture that surprise; even with complex physical and CAD models it is not always possible to predict, for example, the sensation of natural light changing the mood in a space. The experience of the interior spaces and how they connect cannot fully be understood until the building is finished. Once completed, the success of any piece of architecture will rest upon two key factors: does the building suit its intended purpose, and does it respond well to the initial brief?

THE FINISHED GALLERY

6a Architect's expansion of the South London Gallery has been a great success. The café on the ground floor, exhibition spaces on the first floor and flat for the artist-in-residence on the second, have all been incorporated into the rich life of the museum. Behind the house, the three-storey extension creates a double-height room that leads to a link-back to the gallery through the new garden room, effectively joining the two buildings.

At the rear of the site, the Clore Studio is a generous single volume, topped by a central lantern. It develops themes from the house with an exposed roof structure to create calmness and warmth. Like so much at the South London Gallery, the overall simplicity of the space hides some surprises: the west wall pivots to open a continuous field between the back garden and the interior. At night the walls and shutters close the whole building down into an abstract dark box.

Overall, the South London Gallery responds well to its brief; the client is pleased with its sensitive response to the existing building and to the new facilities that have been provided. The scheme creates a carefully considered series of new spaces to allow visitors to appreciate the artwork of the gallery.

1. The Clore Education Studio
The new education building includes a
pivoting wall, which connects the inside of
the building to the garden.

Conclusion

Architecture is everywhere around us, it frames the spaces where we work, live and exist. Architecture is not just about the individual buildings, but about the spaces between and around them and the cities they are part of. Technology and materials inform architecture in terms of construction and making buildings. This is a dynamic environment where the substance of our buildings is constantly changing as well as the expectations we have for architecture.

This book is designed to provide a window into the ways that architects think, consider and design buildings. It involves incredible vision and collaboration at many levels to make a piece of architecture. Architects are passionate about designing new spaces and places and adapting existing buildings and places too.

It takes a great deal of creative energy and enthusiasm to make good architecture. The journey is exciting and the experience of the best pieces of architecture can be inspirational.

1. Flower Towers
David Mathias, 2002
This image brings together a range of architectural thinking and expression.
It has been created using computer modelling and freehand drawing, and
includes a plan, a perspective drawing and a strip elevation across an
urban site.

Bibliography

Ambrose, G., Harris, P. and Stone, S. (2007)
The Visual Dictionary of Architecture
AVA Publishing

Anderson, J. (2010)
Basics Architecture 03: Architectural Design
AVA Publishing

Baker, G. (1996)
Design Strategies in Architecture: An Approach to the Analysis of Form
Von Nostrand Reinhold

Ching, F. (2002)
Architectural Graphics
John Wiley & Sons

Ching, F. (1995)
Architecture, Space, Form and Order
Von Nostrand Reinhold

Clark, R. and Pause, M. (1996)
Precedents in Architecture
John Wiley & Sons

Crowe, N. and Laseau, P. (1984)
Visual Notes for Architects and Designers
John Wiley & Sons

Cullen, G. (1994)
Concise Landscape
The Architectural Press

Curtis, W. (1996)
Modern Architecture Since 1900
Phaidon

Deplazes, A. (2005)
Constructing Architecture
Birkhauser

Farrelly, L. (2007)
Basics Architecture 01: Representational Techniques
AVA Publishing

Farrelly, L. (2008)
Basics Architecture 02: Construction + Materiality
AVA Publishing

Fawcett, P. (2003)
Architecture Design Notebook
The Architectural Press

Le Corbusier (1986)
Towards a New Architecture
Architectural Press

Littlefield, D. (2007)
Metric Handbook: Planning and Design Data (Third Edition)
The Architectural Press

Marjanovic, I. and Ray, K.R. (2003)
The Portfolio: An Architectural Press Student's Handbook
The Architectural Press

Porter, T. (2004)
Archispeak
Routledge

Porter, T. (1999)
Selling Architectural Ideas
Spon Press

Rasmussen, S. (1962)
Experiencing Architecture
M.I.T. Press

Richardson, P. (2001)
Big Ideas, Small Buildings
Thames & Hudson

Robbins, E. (1994)
Why Architects Draw
M.I.T. Press

Sharp, D. (1991)
The Illustrated Dictionary of Architects and Architecture
Headline Book Publishing

Unwin, S. (1997)
Analysing Architecture
Routledge

von Meiss, P. (1990)
Elements of Architecture
E & FN Spon Press

Weston, R. (2004)
Materials, Form and Architecture
Laurence King Publishing

Weston, R. (2004)
Plans, Sections and Elevations
Laurence King Publishing

Webography

The American Institute of Architects
www.aia.org
This website has information about the education and practice of architecture in the USA.

archINFORM
www.archinform.net
This database for international architecture, originally emerging from records of interesting building projects from architecture students, has become the largest online database about worldwide architects and buildings from past to present.

Architecture Link
www.architecturelink.org.uk
Architecture Link aims to be the first port of call for all those interested in the subject of architecture and design. Its main objective is to foster public appreciation of architecture and the built environment, and also to provide a means for easily disseminating information on architecture and design.

Getty Images
www.gettyimages.com
This site makes available many images and visuals that can complement architectural presentation ideas.

Google Earth
www.earth.google.com
Google Earth combines satellite imagery and maps to make available the world's geographic information. Maps can be accessed to provide specific information about any site in the world at varying scales.

Great Buildings
www.greatbuildings.com
This is an architecture reference site that provides three-dimensional models, plans and photographic images of hundreds of international architects and their work.

International Union of Architects
www.uia-architectes.org
The UIA is an international non-governmental organisation founded in Lausanne in 1948 to unite architects from all nations throughout the world, regardless of nationality, race, religion or architectural school of thought. The UIA is a unique world network uniting all architects.

Perspectives
www.archfilms.com
A Chicago-based resource, Perspectives produces high-quality videos on architecture and design. It also creates specialized videos and products for tourism planning, development firms, historic preservation agencies, cultural institutions and communities.

Royal Institute of British Architects (RIBA)
www.architecture.com
The RIBA website provides reference information and advice about the practice and training of architects.

SketchUp
www.sketchup.com
SketchUp is a piece of software that quickly creates a three-dimensional model of a building. It is an easy to use, intuitive program that produces models that look like they have just been sketched freehand.

Glossary

Acontextual
Buildings or ideas that deliberately react against their location in terms of material and/or form can be described as acontextual.

Anthropomorphic
Refers to the application of human characteristics or ideas to animals, natural elements and inanimate objects or forms.

Brise soleil
A device that is used to reduce the sunlight entering a building and is applied to the building façade.

Collage
Collage derives from the French term *coller* (to stick). It was a technique that cubist artists, such as Picasso, used in the 1920s. Collage can be applied to architectural concepts that use elements or references from other ideas, to create a new architectural piece.

Computer-aided design (CAD)
Computer-aided design is the use of computers and specially designed software to design and develop architecture and produce architectural representation.

Concept
This can be described as an initial idea that informs the development of the architectural design. The best concepts can be read clearly at the end of the architectural project in the detail, the plan and the overall interpretation of the building.

Context
In architectural terms, context refers to the setting or placing of the architecture.

Figure ground
The idea of looking at maps of a city that reveal the figure or form of buildings as separate entities from the ground or space around them. It is a concept most famously used by Nolli in Rome in 1748. This allowed spaces to be read in cities separately from the buildings around them.

Free Plan
This concept originates from Le Corbusier and reflects his idea of using a frame structure for building: the Dom-ino frame. This liberates the internal spaces and allows elements such as walls to be located freely within the plan.

Genius loci
This term refers to the spirit or essence of place. A piece of architecture can relate positively to the genius loci.

Hierarchy
In architectural application a hierarchy is an ordering of space, idea or form. Spaces can have more or less relative importance in a plan or building. Making spaces or elements physically larger or smaller suggests relative importance.

Layering
Layers can explain architecture at many levels. Physically, spaces can be designed as layers so that one moves from the outside of a building through to the inside spaces and identifies each layer separately from another. Modernist spaces, such as the Barcelona Pavilion, attempt to break down layers between inside and outside space.

Metaphor
Architectural metaphors are used at the concept stage of designing buildings. Le Corbusier has used the phrase 'a building as a machine for living'. Some metaphors are associated with form and others are more derivative.

Sophisticated metaphors as concepts are subtle rather than literal. A building inspired by a boat will not necessarily resemble a boat physically. It may, however, have boat-like references to material, shape and manufacture.

Module
Modules or measuring systems are essential in architecture. A module could be a brick or a human hand or a millimetre. It needs to be consistent and recognizable. Le Corbusier's *Le Modulor* uses geometry and anthropometrics to create a proportional measuring system.

Order
This refers to the range of classical columns; the five orders are Doric, Ionic, Corinthian, Tuscan and Composite.

Parti
This represents a drawing which reduces an architectural idea to a diagram as a plan, section and/or elevation. The essence of this drawing is that the diagram is simple; it identifies the key issues of the architectural idea.

Piloti

This was used by Le Corbusier and is a French term to describe the columns that raise a building off the ground.

Place

For architecture, place is more than a site or location of a building. A place has physical definitions, it exists somewhere and can be described as geographical coordinates and map references. However, 'place' is about establishing the identity of a location or site, describing spiritual and emotional aspects of the site. Architects are involved in creating 'places', using the physical site as a platform.

Prefabrication

Fabrication describes the process of making objects in a controlled environment, such as a factory. Prefabrication involves the making of large-scale elements that can then be brought to a building site and assembled. These elements can range in scale from a kitchen or bathroom, to a house. Prefabrication allows quick installation and quality control, however it involves large amounts of planning and programming of installation.

Promenade

An architectural promenade derives from Le Corbusier and his idea of a controlled sequenced journey through a building that can act as an architectural device. It provides an order, axis and direction to the architectural idea.

Proportion

Describes the pleasing relationship between elements of an architectural idea or a building design and the whole. Proportioning systems were used in the classical and Renaissance period that related to the human body and the application of geometry.

Scale

Scale is about understanding the relative size of buildings and elements in recognized systems. Drawings and other information have to be prepared to recognized scales to allow buildings to be understood and built. These scales are expressed as a proportion of full size and are usually in metric or imperial.

Serial Vision

In *The Concise Townscapes* (1961), Gordon Cullen refers to the idea of expressing movement through a city as a series of views or serial vision, to allow an idea of a journey to be described as views or sketch perspectives. It is a very useful device to describe a large building or urban space from an experiential point of view.

Servant / served

Louis Kahn used this term to describe the contrasting types of space in architecture. The servant spaces are functional, housing services such as lifts, stairs, toilets, kitchens, ventilation units, heating systems and corridors. Served spaces are those that are experienced and celebrated, the living spaces of a house, the exhibition spaces of a gallery. There is a clear hierarchy between these spaces.

Storyboarding

This is a technique used in comic strip and film design to explain a narrative or story as a series of images or stills. It is a very useful planning device for architects to use to sequence an idea or concept of a building and allows them to plan a visual presentation or a journey though a series of designed spaces.

Tectonic

'Tectonics' describes the science of construction. Technology applies to all ideas of construction and manufacture.

Threshold

Originally the idea of crossing a threshold was to step into a space or territory, as a threshold represents a transition from one space to another. Usually the transition is from inside to outside, but it can be used to describe definitions between internal spaces. Thresholds are normally identifiable and marked; traditionally this was by a stone step, but a change or exaggeration of material at ground level identifies the threshold point.

Typology

This refers to classifications or models of understanding and description. In architecture buildings tend to belong to certain groups; these can be associated with form, function or both. Housing, schools, civic buildings, galleries, museums can all be described as typologies associated with function.

Wrapping

The way in which a wall can be clearly understood to 'wrap' around a simple space.

Zeitgeist

This literally translates as the 'spirit of the age'. In terms of architecture, it is something that transcends the moment and refers to an idea that is broad and all encompassing culturally.

Zoomorphic

Ideas that are informed by animal shapes are referred to as zoomorphic. They may be inspired by physical forms or by material aspects.

Picture credits

Cover image: Guangzhou Opera House, China by Zaha Hadid Architects. Copyright of GuoZhongHua and courtesy of Shutterstock.com.

Introduction
Page 7, image 1: Copyright Pawel Pietraszewski and courtesy of Shutterstock.com.
Page 8, image 1: Courtesy and copyright of Jan Derwig / RIBA Library Photographs Collection
Page 8, image 2: Courtesy of David Cau.
Page 9, image 3: Courtesy of David Cau.

Chapter One
Page 11, image 1: Courtesy of Ewan Gibson
Page 13, image 1: Courtesy and copyright of Thomas Reichart; image 2: Copyright of Graham Tomlin and Courtesy of Shutterstock.com.
Page 14, image 1: Courtesy of Jim Collings.
Page 15, image 2: Courtesy of Luke Sutton.
Page 16, image 2: Student group project courtesy of University of Portsmouth School of Architecture; image 3 courtesy of Aaron Fox.
Page 17, image 4: Courtesy of Paul Craven-Bartle
Page 18, image 1: Courtesy of Richard Harrison; image 2 courtesy of Luke Sutton and The Urbanism Studio (Portsmouth School of Architecture), 2011.
Page 19, images 3 & 5 courtesy of Rosemary Sidwell; image 4 courtesy of Luke Sutton, Edward Wheeler and Portsmouth School of Architecture.
Page 21, image 1: Courtesy and copyright of Simon Astridge; image 2 courtesy and copyright of Bernard Tschumi Architects.
Page 22, image 1: Courtesy and copyright of Chris Ryder; image 2 courtesy and copyright of Bernard Tschumi Architects
Page 23, image 3: Courtesy and copyright of Adam Parsons.
Page 25, image 1: Courtesy of Richard Rogers Partnership and copyright

Katsuhisa Kida/PHOTOTECA.
Pages 26–29, all images courtesy and copyright of Design Engine Architects.

Chapter Two
Page 33, image 1: Courtesy and copyright of Niall C Bird.
Page 39, image 1: Courtesy and copyright of George Saumarez Smith, ADAM Architecture.
Page 41, image 1: Courtesy of Emma Liddell.
Page 42, image 1: Copyright of Vladimir Badaev and courtesy of Shutterstock.com.
Page 43, image 2 Courtesy of Simon Astridge.
Page 44, image 1 Copyright of Khirman Vladimir and courtesy of Shutterstock.com.
Page 45, image 2: Courtesy and copyright of Niall C Bird.
Page 46, image 1: Courtesy of Martin Pearce.
Page 47, image 2: Copyright of Worakit Sirijinda and courtesy of Shutterstock.com.
Page 48 image 1: Copyright of Andy Linden and courtesy of Shutterstock.com.
Page 49, image 2: Copyright of 1000 Words and courtesy of Shutterstock.com.
Page 51, image 1: Copyright of Pecold and courtesy of Shutterstock.com.
Page 52, image 1: Courtesy and copyright of Niall C. Bird; image 2, Courtesy and copyright of RIBA Library Photographs Collection
Page 53, image 3: Copyright of Miguel(ito) and courtesy of Shutterstock.com.
Page 54, image 1: Le Corbusier, Le Modulor, 1945. Plan FLC 21007. (c) FLC/DACS, 2011. Courtesy of ProLitteris.
Page 55, image 2: Courtesy and copyright of Jan Derwig / RIBA Library Photographs Collection.
Page 56, image 1: Copyright of Ute Zscharnt for David Chipperfield Architects.
Page 57, image 2: Courtesy and copyright of David Chipperfield Architects.
Page 58, image 1: Copyright Stiftung

Preussischer Kulturbesitz / David Chipperfield Architects, photographer: Jörg von Bruchhausen
Page 59, image 2: Copyright Stiftung Preussischer Kulturbesitz / David Chipperfield Architects, photographer: Ute Zscharnt
Page 61, image 1: Courtesy of Melissa Royle and Chris Ryder.

Chapter Three
Page 63, image 1: Copyright of Semen Lixodeev and courtesy of Shutterstock.com.
Page 64, image 1: Copyright of Angelo Giampiccolo and courtesy of Shutterstock.com.
Page 65, image 2: Courtesy of Caruso St John Architects LLP. Copyright Héléne Binet.
Page 66, image 1: Copyright of Jody and courtesy of Shutterstock.com.
Page 67, image 2: Courtesy and copyright of RIBA Library Photographs Collection.
Page 68, image 1: Courtesy of Luke Sutton; image 2 courtesy of Philippa Beames.
Page 69, image 3: Courtesy of Roger Tyrell; image 4 copyright of John Kasawa and courtesy of Shutterstock.com.
Page 70, image 1: Copyright of Michael Stokes courtesy of Shutterstock.com.
Page 73, image 2: Courtesy of Martin Pearce.
Page 74, image 1: Courtesy of Simon Astridge; image 2 copyright of Mike Liu and courtesy of Shutterstock.com.
Page 76, image 1: Courtesy and copyright of David Mathias & Peter Williams.
Page 77, image 2: Copyright of ssguy and courtesy of Shutterstock.com.
Page 79, image 3: Courtesy of Nick Hopper.
Page 81 image 1: Copyright Nito and courtesy of Shutterstock.com; image 2 courtesy of Copyright Godrick and courtesy of Shutterstock.com.
Page 83, image 1: Beddington Zero Energy Development images courtesy and copyright www.zedfactory.com.
Page 85, image 1: Copyright of Carlos

Neto and courtesy of Shutterstock.com; image 2, Copyright of fuyu liu and courtesy of Shutterstock.com.

Pages 86–89, section drawing courtesy and copyright of Foster + Partners. All other photographs courtesy and copyright of Nigel Young/ Foster + Partners

Chapter Four

Page 93, image 1: Courtesy of Natasha Butler and Joshua Kievenaar.

Page 95, image 1: Courtesy of Lucy Smith; image 2 courtesy of Charlotte Pollock; image 3courtesy of James Scrace.

Page 96, image 1: Courtesy of Jonathon Newlyn.

Page 97, image 2: Courtesy of Lucy Smith; image 3 courtesy of Ewan Gibson.

Page 98, images 1 and 2: Courtesy of Serpentine Gallery © Peter Zumthor Photography: Walter Herfst.

Page 99, image 4: Courtesy of Colin Graham.

Page 100 image 1 courtesy of Niall Bird; image 2 courtesy of Tim Millard.

Page 101, images 4 and 5: Courtesy of Gavin Berriman.

Page 104, image 1: Courtesy of Stephen James Dryburgh (FM+P); image 2 courtesy of Lucinda Lee Colegate.

Page 105, image 3: Courtesy of Paul Cashin and Simon Drayson; image 4 courtesy of Luke Sutton; image 5 courtesy of Nick Corrie.

Pages 107–109: All images courtesy and copyright of John Pardey Architects. www.johnpardeyarchitects.com

Page 110, image 1: Courtesy of Jo Wickham; image 2 courtesy of Derek Williams

Page 111, image 3: Courtesy of Paul Craven-Bartle.

Page 113, images 1 & 2, Simon Astridge; image 3 courtesy of Jeremy Davies.

Page 115, image 1: Courtesy of Shaun Huddleston (Studio 2); image 2 courtesy of Owen James French; image 3 courtesy of Enrico Cacciatore.

Page 116, image 1: Courtesy of Ewan Gibson.

Page 117, image 2: Courtesy of Lucy Devereux.

Page 118, image 1: Courtesy of David Holden; image 2 courtesy of Luke Sutton.

Page 119, image 3: Courtesy of Claire Potter.

Page 121, image 1: Courtesy and copyright of David Mathias & Peter Williams; image 2 courtesy of Niall Bird.

Page 124, image 1: Courtesy of Luke Sutton.

Page 127, image 3: Courtesy of Nicola Crowson.

Pages 130–133: All images courtesy of Steven Holl Architects. Copyright Andy Ryan.

Page 135, image 1: Courtesy of Melissa Royle and Chris Ryder.

Chapter Five

Page 137, image 1: Courtesy of Zaha Hadid Architects.

Page 138, image 1: Courtesy of Martin Pearce.

Page 139, images 2 and 3: Courtesy of Martin Pearce.

Page 140, images 1 and 2: Courtesy of Martin Pearce.

Page 141, images 3 and 4: Courtesy of Martin Pearce.

Pages 144-145, image 1: Photographs in the Carol M. Highsmith Archive, Library of Congress, Prints and Photographs Division.

Page 146, image 1: Copyright KarSol and courtesy of Shutterstock.com

Page 147, image 1: Copyright fotokik_dot_com and courtesy of Shutterstock.com; images 2 and 3 courtesy and copyright of Aivita Mateika (4AM).

Page 148, image 1: Courtesy of Zaha Hadid Architects. Copyright Christian Richters.

Page 149, image 2: Courtesy of Robin Walker.

Page 151, image 1: Copyright of Simon Detjen Schmidt and courtesy of Shutterstock.com.

Page 153, image 1: Copyright of Daniel Schweinert and courtesy of Shutterstock.com; image 2 copyright of Giancarlo Liguori and courtesy of Shutterstock.com.

Page 154, image 1: Copyright of Jonathan Noden-Wilkinson and courtesy of Shutterstock.com.

Page 155, image 2: Copyright of Cosmin Dragomir and courtesy of Shutterstock.com.

Pages 156–159:All images courtesy of Zaha Hadid Architects.

Page 161, image 1: Courtesy of Melissa Royle and Chris Ryder.

Chapter Six

All images courtesy and copyright of 6a Architects. Photographs on pages 178 and 181 (c) David Grandorge.

Conclusion

Page 183, image 1: Courtesy and copyright of David Mathias

All reasonable attempts have been made to trace, clear and credit the copyright holders of the images reproduced in this book. However, if any credits have been inadvertently omitted, the publisher will endeavour to incorporate amendments in future editions. Unless otherwise cited all images are courtesy of the author and the University of Portsmouth School of Architecture.

Index (Page numbers in *italics* denote illustrations. Entries in *italics* denote publication and films.)

Index

Acknowledgements

This book required the knowledge and support of a variety of individuals, organizations and resources. Thanks are due to colleagues at the Portsmouth School of Architecture, who have supplied images, references and useful additional information.

Thanks also to 6a Architects for offering to provide the information for the project featured in Chapter 6.

An introductory text is critical to engage people at all levels with architecture. Thank you to Rachel Parkinson, Caroline Walmsley and Brian Morris at AVA Publishing, for another chance to try to explain architecture.

Acknowledgements

Lynne Elvins/Naomi Goulder

Working with ethics

The Fundamentals of Architecture

The subject of ethics is not new, yet its consideration within the applied visual arts is perhaps not as prevalent as it might be. Our aim here is to help a new generation of students, educators and practitioners find a methodology for structuring their thoughts and reflections in this vital area.

AVA Publishing hopes that these **Working with ethics** pages provide a platform for consideration and a flexible method for incorporating ethical concerns in the work of educators, students and professionals. Our approach consists of four parts:

The **introduction** is intended to be an accessible snapshot of the ethical landscape, both in terms of historical development and current dominant themes.

The **framework** positions ethical consideration into four areas and poses questions about the practical implications that might occur. Marking your response to each of these questions on the scale shown will allow your reactions to be further explored by comparison.

The **case study** sets out a real project and then poses some ethical questions for further consideration. This is a focus point for a debate rather than a critical analysis so there are no predetermined right or wrong answers.

A selection of **further reading** for you to consider areas of particular interest in more detail.

Ethics is a complex subject that interlaces the idea of responsibilities to society with a wide range of considerations relevant to the character and happiness of the individual. It concerns virtues of compassion, loyalty and strength, but also of confidence, imagination, humour and optimism. As introduced in ancient Greek philosophy, the fundamental ethical question is: *what should I do?* How we might pursue a 'good' life not only raises moral concerns about the effects of our actions on others, but also personal concerns about our own integrity.

In modern times the most important and controversial questions in ethics have been the moral ones. With growing populations and improvements in mobility and communications, it is not surprising that considerations about how to structure our lives together on the planet should come to the forefront. For visual artists and communicators, it should be no surprise that these considerations will enter into the creative process.